God *is* Real

The Miracles That Built My Faith.

ERSILIA FRANCO

WESTBOW
PRESS®
A DIVISION OF THOMAS NELSON
& ZONDERVAN

WestBow Press books may be ordered through booksellers or by contacting:

WestBow Press
A Division of Thomas Nelson & Zondervan
1663 Liberty Drive
Bloomington, IN 47403
www.westbowpress.com
844-714-3454

Scripture quotations are taken from the Holy Bible, New Living Translation, copyright © 1996, 2004, 2007 by Tyndale House Foundation. Used by permission of Tyndale House Publishers, Inc., Carol Stream, Illinois 60188. All rights reserved.

ISBN: 978-1-9736-9910-1 (sc)
ISBN: 978-1-9736-9911-8 (hc)
ISBN: 978-1-9736-9912-5 (e)

Library of Congress Control Number: 2023909647

Print information available on the last page.

WestBow Press rev. date: 06/14/2023

Purpose

To share my testimony about the reality of a living God who is active in my life. I also want to show that miracles are everywhere—if we simply choose to see them. Even in our most challenging moments, the God of the universe never abandons us. If we seek Him and have faith in Him, He'll reward us with endless miraculous acknowledgments of His never-ending love.

Motivation

I was inspired by Eric Metaxas and his book *Miracles*. In particular, I love this single statement, which still blows my mind every single time I read it, because it's just that good.

> Like every miracle that ever was, it is a sign from beyond this world, pointing us to the God beyond this world, to the God who came into this world to lead us back to himself and who is himself the way back.[1]

Our planet is a dark, broken place—now more than ever. In bright contrast, God is alive, and His promises are true. Had my life gone as I planned, I might never have felt His real presence or seen and experienced the magnificent love and care He continues to lavish over me and my family. These stories, the miracles and messages, are real. I don't deserve the number of "burning bush" moments I've received, but

---

[1] Eric Metaxas, *Miracles: What They Are, Why They Happen, and How They Can Change Your Life* (New York: Penguin, 2014), page number.

I am grateful daily for each reminder that I am a spiritual being having an earthly journey. My journey will one day end in heaven.

This world is not my home, at least not in the long run.

Contents

Introduction

I've attended a Calvary Chapel-based church located just south of Nashville, Tennessee for the past twenty years. I've been to two churches in my life: a Catholic church from birth until age thirty-six and a non-denominational, spirit filled, hands in the air, decidedly not Catholic church that would be considered very evangelical. That might sound like two extremes, but it really isn't. I felt completely comfortable from the first time I showed up because of the symmetry in values and theology (at least around the things that matter). I have to admit I still say *mass*, *altar*, and *priest*, but our pastor knows what I mean. He was raised Catholic as well.

I don't remember a time when I didn't believe in God or couldn't feel His presence in my life. Not uncommon for Italians, my mother was the spiritual head of our big family. She too felt God's presence, even as a small child. For my mother, it was a wonderful cloak of protection for a child raised in chaos. She knew who she was in Christ.

Faith is defined as the "substance of things hoped for, the evidence of things not seen" (Hebrews 11:1). For some people, faith happens naturally, and child-like faith remains intact into adulthood. However, trauma and the ravages of life smother and suppress the faith woven into our human DNA. Regardless of where you may be on your own spiritual journey, faith must still be nurtured while we walk this earth. It helps us stay the course and continue our marches toward heaven.

My early understanding of miracles was mainly historic during the first thirty-six years of my life. I, of course, knew about the loaves and fishes and water into wine New Testament Jesus stories. Let's not forget the trauma detailed in the miracles associated with the Catholic saints (often ending in horrible, bloody, painful martyrdom). As a child, I received ongoing and regular religious instruction within my family and through twelve years of Catholic school. We were trained to be responsible. We were told to never ask God for anything for ourselves, because He was consumed with the needs of the less fortunate. We should consider ourselves most certainly fortunate. Jesus was to be adored, but it was understood He too was busy with starving babies in third world countries, so we should turn to our patron saints or the Blessed Mother with our concerns. I did know that our relatives, who had gone before us, could intercede on our behalf and actively hear our prayers. After my grandmothers were gone, I would often speak to them, certain they were much better off and could see and hear me. However, I didn't really consider or even wonder if something as supernatural as miracles was happening to regular people today.

During most of my life, I had the distinct feeling I was on my own. Success or failure was completely in my hands, and failure and asking for help were not options. That character defect was going to cause serious issues as I grew into adulthood. I didn't really believe God had time for me or that I deserved any miracles. Unfortunately, after a blessed childhood, my years as a young wife and mother became extremely difficult. I held on to my Catholic faith like a life raft, neither growing nor fading in my beliefs. In truth, I was barely treading water. I didn't know how badly I needed a miracle, or God's active presence directing my life. I would have turned over control, if I had known that was even an option. Thankfully, today I know Jesus was there all the time. It was me who pushed Him out of the way, trying to do it all myself.

What is a miracle?

Max Turner, a professor of the New Testament at London Bible College, uses the term in the semi-technical sense. It is an event that combines the following traits: it is an extraordinary or startling observable event; it cannot reasonably be explained in terms of human abilities or other known forces in the world; it is perceived as a direct act of God; and it is usually understood to have symbolic or sign value (e.g., pointing to God as redeemer and judge).[2]

Like so many Christians, I viewed God as remote from this world and my daily existence. It was at my new church where I first heard how actively He wanted to involve himself in the small and big things in my life. It took practice for me to humble myself, ask for His guidance, and then trust the process. To be honest, I still work on that daily.

2

I've shared my testimony as a member of Al-Anon and Celebrate Recovery over the past twenty years more than once. The facts of my life are a cautionary tale at best. There are contrasts in my personal story, the terrible things that happened to me and my family, and the truly miraculous, amazing things we have experienced. I don't ignore the bad for the good. They both have their significance. In seasons of extreme duress, it is easy to forget or deny the miraculous. I try to stay in the moment where God meets me, neither pretending the difficulties are not happening or missing the amazing events that occurred in the heart of my deepest despair.

This book is a compilation of twelve miracles, messages, and moments that the God of the universe engineered just for me and my family. Those twelve distinct experiences have built my faith, and helped me wade through some very dark and difficult times. They've helped me to overcome my fear of not having enough, being alone, and even the fear of death. I am most certainly still a work in progress. However, every day is a new opportunity to share what I've learned and experienced and what I know to be true. Putting these stories together is something I felt called to do, to share with someone else out there who might be feeling (as I had) that God was busy with bigger problems.

Everyone can use a message from God; miracles breathe life into faith and sustain us. Faith helps us stay the course. Faith, however, does not mean we will avoid suffering. In fact, as most Christians know, the more you develop spiritually, the more likely it is you'll have more turmoil in your life, not less. The objective isn't to avoid trouble, but rather to not let it break you when the inevitable occurs. God will be there, right beside you, pouring His incredible love and protection over your life. I use the term *miracle*, but God messages or moments are appropriate as well. These are personalized experiences created just for us by a God who understands human pain and suffering.

Everything I've written is true, but the names have been changed to protect the privacy of those involved. These experiences were witnessed by me and others. I call these stories my "burning bush" moments. Did you know that those are not just for Moses? In fact, they are available for everyone, including you.

The Bible validated it, but my own experience sealed the deal.

> Faith shows the reality of what we hope for; it is the evidence of things we cannot see. Through their faith, the people in days of old earned a good reputation By faith we understand that the entire universe was formed at God's command, that what we now see did not come from anything that can be seen. (Hebrews 11:1–3 NLT)

Miracle 1

Believe

It was 2003. My youngest child, a sweet, chubby boy named Archie, was barely two years old. Born just before 9/11, Archie was a source of deep joy from the minute I felt his presence and saw his smile.

However, if I'm being honest, Archie should never have been born.

My marriage was on the rocks and had been for some time. But for a few sunny months in the summer of 2000, when I believed (because I wanted to believe) we were really, really, really going to make it this time, I convinced myself another child would complete our family. My husband and I agreed, and once again, I was able to get pregnant almost immediately. Looking back, I can see clearly that he and I were both unwell and had no right to drag another child into our family of four. However, after a relaxing vacation, caution was thrown to the wind on St. Simon's Island off the coast of Georgia, and we soon discovered Archie was on the way. Unfortunately, those eight months were some of the most challenging of my life. It was clear, as my first trimester ended, that my marriage was failing. My husband was an addict in every sense of the word, and I was likely to experience pre-term labor. I was more than unnerved about the real likelihood that I was going to raise three young children alone, keep a roof over our heads, and try to rebuild my savings and retirement.

Unfortunately, that projection was incredibly accurate. Just two years later, as I turned thirty-eight years old, my marriage was in complete tatters, and survival with my children, ages two, six, and ten, had become the epicenter of my universe. Life as I'd known it was about to change forever. We were on the verge of divorce after years of my tolerating addiction, infidelity, and emotional abuse. I was hopeless and fearful; it was a true low point in my life. I considered myself a "tough chick" in so many ways, and most people who thought they knew me would corroborate that statement. Outside of my thriving career, everything else in my life was broken. Coming to grips with the fact that my dream of an intact family and the hope for a fiftieth anniversary were over was crushing. Seventeen years prior, on a beautiful September day, in a military wedding with the Blue Angels streaking across the sky over Latrobe, Pennsylvania, I had been so confident of a bright and happy future. However, we had failed—more specifically, I had failed—and it was more than I could bear.

As I wrote in my diary in that moment, "I am afraid of my husband." I couldn't even say it out loud, but it was true.

Behind closed doors, there was chaos in our home, loaded weapons under our bed, bottles and drugs hidden in the garage and house, and strange people making appointments for "legal help" who paid for services rendered in cash, weapons, and drugs. The father of my children was ill, deathly ill, and his disease was killing me a little bit every day. I would open the door after work, two young girls and a baby boy tucked behind me, because I was never certain what I would find inside. Threats of suicide were a constant reminder that I had to be diligent and I had to protect the kids. If I couldn't find a way to stop it, then I too might die.

I'd nearly given up, but through the help of a co-worker and another positive upswing in my husband's mental state, we found our way to a last-ditch effort to save the marriage and his life. We were at a nondenominational church in Leiper's Fork, Tennessee. I was still deeply Catholic at the time and the girls were in Catholic school. In better moments, my husband would want to go to church, any church, other than a Catholic one. In the closing moments of our marriage, I would have willingly gone to a Buddhist temple if I thought it would save him. However, this place was different. It was warm and inviting and everyone seemed happy, like they really wanted to be there. We were invited to a Sunday service by a co-worker's wife, and the sermon was a demonstration about marriage using clay and a potter's wheel. I felt exposed, like everyone knew it was just for us. As a Catholic, I still went to mass every week too. I could do that on Saturday evening, checking the box, getting credit for the ritual. After a few months, and another downturn, our problems led us to reach out to the pastor. He had walked up to me at that very first service and said, "I know you. Four-year-old soccer, right?" A picture flashed in my mind: a dad with a cool bracelet made of smooth stones watching his tall, athletic daughter mow down the other kids. I remember thinking that he must be a music person from Los Angeles, a common persona in Nashville, but a pastor? Now that was unexpected.

I continued to go to this nondenominational church. That simple act of showing up felt like hope, a final effort to save what we'd created and save his life, while finding sanity for myself. After yet another relapse, and a refusal to seek the help necessary to stay sober, the writing was finally on the wall. I knew I couldn't break free of the marriage without a spiritual "get out of jail free" card, and I didn't feel comfortable that the Catholic church would be supportive. Transparency in general had not worked very well for me thus far. At this point, my oldest was gearing up for her confirmation. One day she said, "Mom, I know what this means, and I don't want to be an adult member of this church. Let's go to the new church." I couldn't argue. It is amazing how children soak in truth like sponges, even when they don't know the entire story of what is going on with the adults in their lives.

Divorce.

I hated the word; the label that would stigmatize my children and myself forever. Although it was needed and necessary, I still craved approval from a spiritual source to allow me to entertain thoughts of escape. I couldn't believe God would be okay with me doing anything but giving 1000 percent to fix things, a daily grind of trying to get him to sober up and pursue recovery, forgive again all the lies and infidelities. Clearly, I didn't think God thought much of me. I was failing, and that was simply unacceptable.

During that time, on a Sunday morning before anyone was awake, a soft thud bumped my mother's intuition back online. The baby was up. He was not a climber like most boys. He preferred to wait patiently in his crib until I walked in the room. The moment I opened the door would always cause a huge smile to spread across his fat cheeks. The pure joy radiating from this little guy kept me alive. That morning, the thud was followed by the sound of chunky feet moving quickly across the old wood floor. He was coming toward us quickly—how odd. I couldn't remember a single time that this had happened, so I sat up in bed rubbing my eyes as the door slowly opened. My husband then rolled over and said, "Archie, what are you doing?."

Sidebar: I come from a long line of baby talkers. No Franco worth his or her salt would ever consider speaking to a baby like an adult. Mom trained us in a baby language that I can still turn on and off easily. My six siblings and I all do it, along with making up silly nicknames for our kids. Archie's other name was Nee Nee Tollinsworth. Don't ask why, that was just part of the Franco deal. At two, he was speaking with a sweet baby gibberish that included words like 'nuggle for snuggle, as in "Mommy can we 'nuggle?" It was honestly too cute for this world. He didn't speak like an adult. He didn't have to as far as I was concerned. I wanted to freeze him just at that age. He was clearly filling a big emotional need for me at that time.

Back to the miraculous message: He crawled up over the end of our bed, another strange thing for him to do. He then sat down on his diapered bottom, seeming to compose himself while we stared at him our mouths open. He then reached both of his arms out with tiny chubby hands open and extended, looked us right in the eyes, and said, "Believe" as clear as a bell—just like an adult. We were sleepy but the clarity of his voice and the word he never used before had us both sitting up at attention with open mouths, unable to process what we were both hearing. His father then said, "Archie, what did you say?"

Again, Archie looked down, composed himself, then looked up at us, reached out his arms and in an adult voice said, "Believe." He then rolled off the bed and went running out of our room, babbling like a two-year-old.

I grabbed my husband and said, "You heard that. We both heard that." He acknowledged that he had as I thought, *I'll lose it if he disagrees with me.* I jumped out of bed and twirled around. "Did you hear that? That was a word from God!" In my own head I thought, *Wow, you sound like one of those overly exuberant folks at our new church.* In contrast, my husband was not ready to go there as quickly. As a Catholic, this sort of thing was completely unheard of; miracles always involved bloody tears, a saint's bone, or cloud formations, not pudgy, barely twenty-two-month-old baby boys. I was so excited, but I wanted a third party to validate what I just heard, explain what on earth it meant, and then confirm that Archie was clearly a baby prophet.

I got ready for church and, as I showered and dressed, I had a feeling of peace and happiness that I had not felt in a long time. Sadly, my husband was unwilling to come to church that morning. However, I couldn't wait to get to there to tell Pastor Sam and his wife Heather what had happened. I knew it was a safe environment for that type of conversation. After service, I found Sam entertaining questions and feedback from other church members. I waited my turn and then, like a little kid on Christmas morning, said, "Guess what? Guess what?" I then relayed the entire story to him in great detail while he patiently listened, absorbing what I shared without any reaction. I so badly wanted to know if this was a sign from God that my marriage would be saved. I thoroughly expected the pastor to be shocked or surprised. With a straight face, not finding this in any way unusual, all he said was, "Well, let's see if he is willing to listen." I'm not sure I would have called this a miracle. I'm not certain I even believed in miracles at that point in my journey. Every ounce of energy was focused on saving my husband. I was, and am, a classic codependent. What I didn't know then was that this message from the God of the universe, shared by a two-year-old baby boy, was not just for my husband. It was for me too.

How amazing. How incredible. The child who I had no business bringing into this world shared a heavenly message, designed for me and his father.

> God will take our messes and transform them into miracles. Isaiah 61:3 reminds us that God will give us "a crown of beauty for ashes, a joyous blessing instead of mourning, festive praise instead of despair" (NLT)

Miracle 2

"When You Shibured"

Fast forward just a few years. Archie, still delicious and chubby, was now in pre-school. He remained sweet and agreeable and would stay close to me as I went about my day without complaint. I was by this time divorced; my husband walked out the door on my thirty-ninth birthday, the day before our seventeenth anniversary. I wasn't sad. Honestly, I was incredibly relieved. How did I get there? Well, I distinctly remember a phone call I received from my pastor about six months earlier. He asked me to come to the church. I wasn't sure what he was going to say, but I knew that my life was about to change one way or another. As I walked in the door and sat down, he quietly composed himself. The silence was deafening. He then said, "You need to get out of this marriage, and we're here to help." A flood of relief washed over me. I broke down in tears. I knew it was time. I needed that spiritual approval because the guilt and shame I felt was so acute. He kindly reminded me that I was not Jesus, and I was not meant to sacrifice myself for my husband. Jesus loved my husband and would love him even when we were no longer married.

I had done all that I could possibly do to hold the marriage together for almost two decades and it was time to let him go.

My focus going forward was taking care of three kids and somehow forgiving both me and my ex-husband for the harm this would cause them. I spent many hours in recovery meetings (Al-Anon) trying to find the woman who felt so sane and good seventeen years prior. Reinventing yourself at almost forty is no small feat, but I was grateful to no longer have the weight or ownership of someone else's salvation on my back. It was a burden I could no longer bear.

Once my story was out and I became the "hard-working divorced mom of three," it was amazing how many women in similar circumstances came into my life. It was the beginning of understanding that my pain and suffering would be of more benefit to the world than the veneer of perfection I had so carefully crafted over the years. After all, every bit of it was a lie, right down to the white picket fence.

My new life, with all the warts, was a calling card for authenticity to others. I was becoming more empathetic to difficult circumstances and wounding as I accepted the failure in myself. I needed God; I was no longer a one-women wrecking machine. I was broken but accessible. I had no idea how much stress was created keeping up the "happy life" charade or how relaxing authenticity could be.

Every morning, I was doing my best to get Archie to daycare, the girls to grade school, and myself to work. The beginning of each day was pure chaos, but the time in the car was also an opportunity to talk to the girls while we nibbled on treats from Starbucks and drank hot chocolate that Lauren would invariably spill. Around that time, I was asked to provide some content for a work newsletter offering a suggestion for making mornings easier. I made the mistake of admitting that I would put the baby into his outfit for the next day at bedtime so I could just get him up and get out the door. That brought howls from my boss, a wealthy man with a stay-at-home wife who had no sense of just how challenging my life had become. However, I stuck to my guns with the Pop-Tart crumbs and chocolate stains strewn across the backseat and continued on. I was doing the best I could, and that had to be good enough.

Catholic school was not tolerant of chronic lateness, evangelicals, or single moms. I needed help—something else that recovery was teaching me to acknowledge. There was a mom at school with four little girls, two of whom were the same age as Matilda and Lauren. She was super mom in my eyes. She was there for her kids, served lunches in the cafeteria, and had a husband who took photos at all the sporting events. In my mind, they were tiny and perfect, like wedding cake toppers. Much to my surprise, their marriage soon fell apart, and I rushed to her side to support her through the divorce process. She would take my girls to her house when I couldn't get there on time for after school pick-up. Every Wednesday, I brought a bottle of wine and a giant pizza to her house for dinner. We would talk, she would smoke, and the kids would run all over the place, sweating in the heat of the Indian summer.

One day, I received word that my friend had a seizure. She was so thin, so small, and struggling. I knew she was not being healthy. I tried to talk and walk her through the misery of divorce, continuously sharing that there was hope and life on the other side. After the seizure, she could no longer drive, so our visits became more frequent. One night, we walked into her kitchen, big hot pizza box in one hand and Archie holding on to the other. She and I were talking after the kids had plowed through most of the pie, when we noticed that Archie had joined us. He walked up to her, grabbed her hand, and said, "Miss Sarah." She looked down at him and he cleared his little throat and said again, "Miss Sarah."

She then replied, "Yes Archie?"

Again, he composed himself, like I'd seen him do that Sunday morning a few years earlier. He then looked up with that pudgy face and said, "When you fell on the floor and shibured (shivered), it made God really sad."

Archie didn't know about the seizure. However, it turned out he knew about something much bigger. A few weeks later, I stopped by her house on my way home from work and she and the girls were gone. I was so confused. We had plans and she was nowhere to be found. A month later, her ex-husband came to my house. I had not seen or spoken to him in a year. She had told me some terrible things about what he did to her and why he left. It turned out that none of that was true. He calmly shared that she was in rehab for alcohol addiction and he had temporary custody of the kids. He then explained that the seizure was the result of her trying to stop drinking on her own. I was so blown away that I had missed it. After all I'd been through, I felt like I had a master's degree in substance use disorder, and yet, I totally misjudged the situation. God didn't miss it, and he spoke directly to her through my son in that earlier moment. After Archie left the kitchen, she fell to her knees and cried. I realized after talking to her husband that God convicted her in that moment. The God of the universe wanted her to stop, repent, and turn back to Him.

God speaks to us through the Bible, prayer, dreams, pastors, worship, and even through children, if we would only stop and listen. It really is amazing. It reminded me once again that we are all sinners, we all need Jesus, and Jesus never gives up on us no matter how far from Him we move. I've witnessed this in my former husband's struggles, my children's struggles, and most certainly my own.

God literally chases us down because He loves us that much.

> "If a man has a hundred sheep and one of them wanders away, what will he do? Won't he leave the ninety-nine others on the hills and go out to search for the one that is lost?" (Matthew 18:12 NLT)

Miracle 3

Tithing and Truth

I was terrified. My greatest fear as a newly divorced mom was not being able to provide for my children, to give them a life like the one I experienced. If we were no longer an intact family, then I at least wanted to give them the education I'd received and of course keep a roof over their heads. I stressed constantly about the mortgage payment, the kid's college funds, the stock market, and my retirement, now depleted by 50 percent—another victim of the ravages of divorce. How was I going to cover college, healthcare, and even future weddings? All of it was going to be my responsibility. I knew that even then.

Men often define themselves by what they do. I defined my success based on being able to provide for my kids. Safety and security had been destroyed in the divorce process and I was trying to hang on and rebuild. I was alone and it was all on my shoulders—mine and mine alone. I had always been a planner and a penny pincher. It was my nature. I remember a vacation when I was about eleven years old. I stressed at every dinner we ate in a restaurant, worrying that my father might struggle covering all of it. I don't know why I was infused with that fear from such a young age. Perhaps I sensed my father's stress raising seven children during the 70s and 80s outside of Pittsburgh, Pennsylvania. I had a spreadsheet to project what I needed to earn, spend, and save; it made me feel safe and in control. The divorce stripped away any sense of financial security. It left the kids and me with little savings, drained my retirement, and left me facing a mortgage and expenses that I wasn't certain I could cover. I was stressed, to say the least. It didn't help that during the divorce process, my soon to be ex-husband drained our checking account. I couldn't pay the mortgage and I was literally hysterical. In tears, I called my pastor, who had become a stable touchpoint during the entire process. He called my now ex-husband and in no uncertain terms told him to put the money back. Thankfully, he complied. For someone who was so cautious with money and never lived paycheck to paycheck, this was pushing me to the very limits of my sanity.

Remember, God was busy—in my mind anyway. The possibility of going to Him, even after what I had learned in my journey through recovery and as a newly minted non-denominational Christian, had still not sunk in fully. Worry was my "go to" move. Finally, brought to my knees at the very moment of my divorce, I turned to the Father and asked Him to help me let go of everything and walk through the process that would free me from what would have been a miserable future. Into what, however, I wasn't certain.

We were now officially recovering Catholics and a broken family. At the same time, I was waiting to hear back from a biopsy for a lump found in my right breast. I was literally sitting in the parking lot outside the hospital when the kids' Catholic school called and shared that "I was not giving enough," and therefore they were going to double my tuition for both daughters. They knew I was getting divorced, and they knew the kid's dad had left. I hadn't asked for help, but I had asked the principal and the girl's teachers to be aware of the pressure they were under based on what was happening in their lives. I was crushed and simply couldn't believe the cruel lack of empathy. I had a good Catholic school experience. All seven Francos had attended the same Catholic grade school and high school. My father had sacrificed so much to make that happen, and I was determined to offer my children the same experience. My father happened to call just after I hung up with the school. I was in the middle of my first official anxiety attack spreading in my chest and closing my throat. He offered to help with the additional tuition, which just made me cry even harder. I was failing. I talked to my older sister the next day and, like the warrior woman and protector she is, she called the parish priest and in no uncertain terms let him have it. She never met the young priest, but he likely won't forget her. He, of course, said it was the business office and not he who was behind the phone call and horrible news. Okay.

I decided to leave the Catholic Church and the kids' school in that very moment. I knew I couldn't make the drive and pay the tuition on my own. I was so angry about how my kids were being treated. I needed change, they needed change, and I had to simplify. I later discovered there were several women in the same or similar situation as myself who were being pushed out of the Catholic school. The school board didn't want us; divorce apparently was like a virus that might spread. I was furious. Thankfully, the kids loved our new church family and the children's programs. By then, I felt very comfortable making this our official and sole church home. I called the pastor and demanded a very detailed onboarding process, including ancient papyrus, calligraphy, wax seals, and some sort of pseudo papal blessing. Pastor Sam shared that his church didn't do that. I demanded, "I need something super official." He got it; he was raised Catholic as well. He understood that this was leaving my culture, my family, and my history. But more importantly, what would my mother say?

In the midst of this, I was growing spiritually, and it felt amazing. Al-Anon, combined with a wonderful church family and new friends, was the renewal I needed. Recovery leads to a spiritual awakening, and I was having those moments on a regular basis. I began a regular cadence of dragging my friends to my new church. My neighbor, another single mom, was with me when they announced a weekend event focused on tithing. There was a spiritual subject I knew absolutely nothing about. My parents were very generous and always contributed to the church and causes they cared about. I'm not sure the 10 percent was a Catholic mandate. I never heard anything about tithing and so she and I signed up. I was eager to learn.

This was a Friday night and all-day Saturday event at church—a big commitment for two single moms, but I felt a tug and so we dug in. One of the founders of the Promise Keeper's movement gave the presentation. This pastor had an amazing personal story, combined with a deep and Biblical understanding of tithing. Saturday concluded with a request that all of the 200 or so attendees make a spiritual gift for an unknown cause that would be revealed the next morning during our regular service. For me, the nervous hyper planner who managed and controlled everything, this sort of generosity was not in my wheelhouse. However, motivated by the Spirit, I went all in, writing a check for an amount that was dear to me at that time. It felt good to let go and let God. However, out in the parking lot as the moon was rising over the fields surrounding our church, I again broke down, crying quietly to myself as fear swept over me like a wave that knocks you down and tosses you on the beach. A few feet away I heard a voice say, "Franco!" I turned around to see my pastor coming toward me. He asked what was wrong and I told him the truth. I was afraid. He said, "Franco, I don't know why tithing works, but it does. Just keep doing it." I smiled and pulled myself together. I actually slept well that night.

The next morning at church, Pastor Sam announced the weekend event had been a huge success and a significant amount of money had been collected. He then shared that the church was going to match what we had all given, doubling the impact. The entire amount was going to be given away that morning. As we sang in worship, a buzz was growing as every minute passed. We all waited patiently to hear who was about to be massively blessed.

In 2006, a civilian engineer had gone to Iraq to help rebuild infrastructure. He left Atlanta and his family because he was hoping to fund college for his daughter. Tragically, he was captured and beheaded live on TV. The world watched a grainy video of the sickening murder broadcast around the globe. Our pastor, moved by the spirit, reached out to the family, and asked them to come to our church in the country outside of Nashville, Tennessee. The media was all over this poor family, so the fact that Sam was able to reach them by phone and convince this women and her daughter to come to our church with zero information about why or what was going to happen was miraculous. Our pastor stepped out on faith that whatever we were going to give her was worth their time and effort. As the church waited anxiously, he announced who would receive the gift as this sweet mother and daughter slowly walked up to the altar.

Patti Hensley and her teenage daughter Sara left our church with more than her college tuition. It was a beautiful, glorious display of love for a family that none of us knew. It was God taking what He gave to us and giving it to someone in desperate circumstances. It was just and right. I still remember our pastor jumping and leaping around across the altar in pure joy. It truly is better to give than receive. I was liberated from the fear of not having enough in that very moment, literally in the blink of an eye. I have tithed since that day and will continue until I graduate to my heavenly home.

The good pastor was right (he always is). That freedom from a persistent attitude of scarcity gave me the courage to start a company, something that I'd been encouraged to do by many of my closest friends. I'd been told by a therapist I came to trust implicitly during and after my divorce that I was "unemployable." I took offense naturally, but she explained that she too fell in that category. I was immediately defensive, sharing that I had played college basketball and was a team player. Her response was, "Let me guess: when you are the captain of the team you are a team player, correct?" Wow, that investment in my mental health continued to teach me new things. I took the leap soon after, building a marketing organization from the ground up. I take healthy pride in the fact that it has been a vehicle to replace what was lost and bless my team and their families. I have not been crippled by fear of financial disaster in more than fourteen years. I, of course, do the footwork; I've been responsible, and I work hard. I also know that I am not alone. He is always just ahead, leading me forward to whatever is next. I've committed my company to His glory and our statement of faith is front and center on the website.

I've been blessed beyond my wildest expectations. I have been able to care for my family, and I no longer fear not having enough.

My trust in God, and not myself, has set me free.

> Pure and genuine religion in the sight of God the Father means caring for orphans and widows in their distress and refusing to let the world corrupt you. (James 1:27)

Miracle 4

The Nicaraguan Prophet

My oldest child is smart, beautiful, and fearless.

She was a compliant baby and little girl, almost weirdly so. She had long curly brown hair and looked like a baby doll with a wide face, big blue eyes, and freckles covering her pale little nose. Her white skin was always shocking next to my own, which has an olive hue and tans deeply in the summer. She asked me once when she was five why we were different colors. I said, "Because I'm Italian and you are mostly Irish." That always made us laugh.

This child's life has been marked by both great suffering and incredible miracles.

At just three years of age, she was sleeping in a big girl bed. One evening in the middle of the night, she decided to wake up, turn her lights on, and jump up and down. Perhaps liberated from a crib and in her own room with a window painted on her wall from *Where the Wild Things Are*, she wanted to get a little wild. At some point, she went flying into her dresser and broke her collar bone. Rather than crying out for her parents, which would have been normal, she quietly turned off her light, walked into our room and woke me up to share that her "stomach hurt." I immediately sat her on the potty—the Franco cure for nearly every ill. After a few minutes, she asked to go back to bed. In the morning, she walked into our room again with her shoulder and arm sagging slightly. When I asked what was wrong, she said that she broke her arm. Now I was really confused. We went to the doctor, as it was clear that something was off and we had a real medical issue. There is nothing like having a pediatrician tell you your kid has a broken bone while you stare off into space wondering how on earth that happened. I was waiting for the good doctor to call the Department of Children's Services. A few days later, Matilda finally fessed up to her pre-school teacher about her midnight gymnastics routine. The fact that she came up with a story and was able to hide a broken bone showed both an amazing pain tolerance and serious manipulation skills.

A year later, she contracted E. coli and literally didn't complain until it was so obvious something was terribly wrong because she started to literally bleed from her backside. Yet again, she barely complained, only mentioning once again that she had a stomachache. A young pediatrician rushed us to Vanderbilt Children's Hospital and likely saved her life. She spent a week in isolation, suffering quietly with no pain medication. It was a horrible time, but as I walked around the floor, I would often see kids in the midst of cancer treatment who were also suffering. I would pray for them and focus on being grateful that this was going to pass and focus on the fact that she was receiving excellent care. I also relied heavily on regular communication with my six brothers and sisters, who called regularly until my husband disconnected the phone, unplugging my support system.

Thankfully, she recovered fully.

As she approached her twelfth birthday and our divorce process was well underway, her pediatrician discovered that her slight scoliosis had progressed alarmingly. Even after a year and a half of being subjected to the discomfort of a full body night brace, there was no improvement—her body continued to twist cruelly. She was now 60 percent off at the top of her back and 40 percent at the bottom. When she bent over, I could see the S that was her spine. "How much more God?" I would cry at night. There was no solution other than a massive surgery involving fileting her along the entire length of her spine, adding two titanium rods, many clips, and screws—a literal internal erector set. Her father had already moved out, but we agreed to drive her to Vanderbilt together for an early surgery on a very cold winter morning with snowflakes peppering the car's windshield. My Al-Anon sponsor, a wonderful older woman who was my hero and cheerleader, met me there so I didn't have to sit alone with the man who walked out on us. I was hurting emotionally and second-guessing my decision to take a perfectly healthy child into a hospital for a radical surgery. My sponsor cracked jokes and kept me distracted as minutes turned into hours.

When we were brought back to see her post-op, the surgeon showed us the image of her back, smiling broadly and pleased with the relatively straight-line he had created. I stared in horror as my stomach lurched. I'm not squeamish but that metal looked like a cage inside her body, trapping her permanently in an upright position. It was more than I could bare. She, once again, rarely complained, even as they insisted she sit up early the next day. It was bravery on a new level. As uncomfortable as it was to share emotional space with her angry, distant father, I knew it was the least I could do. Fortunately, a regular cadence of friends visited to keep me company that week, providing the support and ongoing distraction I needed.

She was not an athletic child, even before the surgery. I played basketball in college and prided myself on athletic prowess. We tried nearly every sport to find something Matilda might love, including swimming, soccer, basketball, and even cross-country. This child was more comfortable reading Harry Potter books than running around and sweating. That surgery ended any remote interest in athletics or any interest in physical activity in general, including gym class in the ninth grade. The girls were asked to run around the gym and a few of them made fun of her awkward gait. She walked out and wouldn't go back. I pulled her out of the public high school and put her in an alternative school called Middle College—think *Breakfast Club* with the freedom to go off campus for lunch and take classes at the community college. She did all of that, even graduating early with about eighteen college credits.

High school was not filled with good memories for my Matilda. As smart as she was and is, the social rigor of teen years, combined with her father leaving and a growing tendency to take massive risks, had her on a path of destruction. I'm sorry to say, but as she nears her twenty-ninth birthday, there are a horrifying number of classmates and friends no longer on this earth. Suicides and drug overdoses have ravaged a generation of bright, creative, wild children. At each new report (one just today as I type this) my heart breaks for yet another soul and the waste of potential.

This child went from baby doll to troubled teen, ricocheting through several schools as I tried desperately to find the right place for her to flourish. There were moments, even at the Catholic school, where special teachers saw in her what I always had: angels sent to push her in a positive direction. A sweet English teacher would quietly place sticky notes on her folders with checklists of what to bring home. In high school, a Spanish teacher became one of her greatest advocates. Matilda would return one day with a master's degree in Central American literature to share the impact this teacher had on her life. However, back then, it was pure chaos. She learned one thing from me: if she just kept her grades up, she could get away with almost anything. My blind spot around performance passed along to another generation. By the grace of God, she graduated, wasn't arrested, hadn't crashed a car, and she was still alive. All in all, I was surviving if not thriving in the parenting game.

Just after her sixteenth birthday, I married my second husband, Fulton. I still call him my "new" husband---he doesn't like that very much, but it's true. We'd been dating for a year, and it was time. I was terrified of committing, of combining checking accounts and, truth be told, of her reaction. My wise therapist shared a strategy for talking to her about it. Trish, one of my heroes, told me in no uncertain terms that this was my decision, and validated that it was done with all the children's collective best interests at heart. She suggested I take my oldest child to a local restaurant where she couldn't escape; it was brilliant. During that time, I had a very strong feeling; I can't say it was as visceral as hearing from heaven, but the message was clear: "Your children need to see a real relationship and a happy marriage before they are on their own." By then I was fully nondenominational and open to that sort of spiritual instruction.

Fulton is a Renaissance man in the purest sense of the word. He has had more successful careers than anyone I've ever known. He had his own radio show during college in Hattiesburg, Mississippi, where he studied journalism at the University of Southern Mississippi. After graduation, he headed to coastal Mississippi to continue his career as a news anchor and radio personality in Biloxi. It was the 70s and early 80s, and there were just three TV stations. Like Ron Burgundy, he was kind of a big deal. From there he made his way to Jackson, the Mississippi state capital, where he entered politics working for the mayor's office as a press secretary. After firing himself in a dramatic protest when asked to lay off a large group of police officers, he was soon recruited by a regional engineering firm where he stayed for fifteen years, retiring as the vice president of business development to become a pastor. See the connection? Neither did he, but God uses all things for good.

Fulton had not been to church his entire life, and neither had his first wife—an unusual situation for a southern couple. They had no preconceived notions about different faiths and just didn't think much about it. However, as they reached mid-life, something stirred in Carol and she found herself at a growing nondenominational church near their home in Bellevue, just outside of Nashville, Tennessee. Fulton admits he had no interest in joining her, and assumed it was a phase that would pass. After several Sundays went by, he began to worry some guy might hit on her so he might as well go as her companion. Not exactly the beginning of a holy attachment, but God was most definitely up to something. After a month or so, Fulton decided to volunteer with the media group, something he was very familiar with through his work experience. That began a relationship with the head pastor and church staff that would lead to a very dramatic conversion, changing both their lives forever. Eventually, the lead pastor asked Fulton to come on board as the executive pastor to manage the daily operations of the church. His family and colleagues were likely shocked by this as it was a 180-degree shift. After a year of untangling himself from a long and successful career, he became a newly minted pastor and gave himself 100 percent to the success of the church. He often shares that God "hijacked" him which is a fairly accurate description of his experience.

Not many years later, as they were planning a trip to Italy for their twentieth anniversary, Carol was diagnosed with Stage 4 ovarian cancer. Fulton shared the only regret he had was that they didn't go, wanting to dive into treatment to save her life. She would struggle through thirty-six months of nonstop chemo and surgeries before succumbing to this awful disease just before her forty-ninth birthday. It was a difficult time. After a painful transition, the church was struggling to find a new lead pastor, and my husband was trying to figure out how to continue his life without the wife he had loved for twenty-three years. An endless stream of baked goods and casseroles arrived at his front door from well-wishing parishioners, many of them single women. Through grief counseling and attending a few groups for people who recently lost spouses, he was getting his sea legs back and began participating in 100-mile distance bicycle races. The peace and comfort that came from training for long rides, along with renovating the home they shared for eighteen years, provided the space necessary to contemplate the future once again.

For some reason, about the same time, I had given up on organically finding a soul mate. Fulton too was looking for something safe and slow that would introduce him back into the dating game. We both tried eHarmony for the first time in 2007. A friend of mine said, "Why not---you aren't doing so well by yourself?" I'd been single for three and a half years at that point, dating and having fun, but with no real prospects who were capable of, or interested in, being stepfathers to two unruly children and an angry teen. I separated my dating life from my role as mom and had been floating along without taking many risks. I was very nervous about introducing anyone to my children, who were still so bruised and battered by the ongoing war with their father exacerbated by the constant rotation back and forth between us. We were moving forward, and it was a level of chaos I felt I could manage.

However, God always has other plans—better plans not ruled by our very real (and reasonable) fears.

So, back to eHarmony. I thought, *Okay, let's go for it!* I dug into filling out an eHarmony profile. I figured this was better than Match.com, and if I was going to do it then I would be the real, authentic me. No pictures, no spin—100 percent Jesus forward. I'd not really done that as I dated in my early forties. Rather than waiting on God, I took the Sadie Hawkins approach and figured I'd just start dating a guy, then drag him into church and devotion to all things Christian through the sheer force of my will. As you might imagine, that was not working very well. I was forever showing up at Sunday service with some poor man on my arm, hoping he would magically become the partner who wanted to be there with me. One Sunday, our pastor literally mouthed, "Who is that?" to me.

My response was to shake my head and say, "Ahhh this guy— no one special." It was not a godly or successful process. My dream was to find a man who wanted to be the spiritual leader of my home, and a father to my kids, a man who would be happy to go to my beloved church with me. However, fear of giving up control was significant and finding that "needle in a haystack" man capable of the type of relationship I wanted felt like a bridge too far. Pushing fear aside, I put all my chips on the table and pressed enter to send my newly minted profile to the great database in the sky. I remember calling this same friend and saying, "Hey I did all the stuff, and nothing is happening." Apparently, it takes a few hours or even days. My impatience was getting the best of me. Given that I refused to add a photo of myself, something that would have kept me from being interested in a conversation, I should not have been surprised. I guess I was a bit shallow in addition to impatient.

Eventually I had a few bites, but they were all a good bit older, and many had that Baptist preacher sort of vibe. Given that I'd only been to the Catholic church and one large evangelical church, all the other flavors were a mystery to me. Then a pleasant looking man with a big, warm smile popped up. He too was older, about nine and a half years north of me, but his profile was well written. It was clear he had loved his first wife until her passing—a spiritually grounded man who didn't leave. Something in my spirit stirred.

His job description said, "Director of Administration." A bit ambiguous, but after a bunch of bad first dates, I was up for almost anything short of "witness relocation program." The last book he'd read (per his profile) was *A Christmas Carol*. Not gonna lie—that too was a bit unusual but certainly not a deal breaker. I was unintentionally coy, communicating back and forth by messaging in the eHarmony system and then email, but not talking or discussing my kids. "Hard to get" was not really my style, but I had no idea if he was really a widower and felt the need to keep a distance until I had confirmed his authenticity. A gal who worked for me at that time, a nurse by day but a private eye at night, did some digging and verified the details of everything he shared, giving me the green light to meet him live and in person. She was very useful during those single years, even calling me one time in the middle of a blind lunch date with the direction to "get up and head to the bathroom and then leave out of the backdoor" after her research had uncovered some disconcerting information. However, Fulton got a clean bill of health.

When Fulton and I finally met in person, more than a month and a half later, it was for dinner in Nashville at what would become one of our favorite places. We closed it down that first night and ended up talking in the parking lot for a few more hours. It was the best date I'd ever had, and we were certainly connecting at a deeper level because we knew one another. We began a courting process that included jogging a few times a week. I'd make him park around the corner and afterward leave quietly. A nosy neighbor who loved my little boy asked me one day who that "good looking man" was that I was running around town with. That made me chuckle. My social life was the talk of the geriatric crowd in downtown Franklin.

After about six months, I asked him to run what became known as "the gauntlet," which involved meeting with an endless string of healthy couples who I trusted to offer feedback and the discernment I didn't have. Everyone was positive—well almost everyone. My pastor and his wife were the final stop of the lengthy interview process. The minute we walked into their home, Sam looked at Fulton and said in a slightly menacing manner, "So, did you like your father?." Oh boy! I quickly ran into the kitchen to speak to Heather. After a night of good steak and conversation, even they seemed super positive, which helped calm my fears. Heather whispered to me as we left that night, "You'll be married in less than a year."

I still did not want to get married, but dating a pastor endlessly was also not going to be an option. Again, I asked God, using all of my recovery skills, to give me courage, and I prayed through it one day at a time.

Fulton and I were married on a hot July afternoon in front of my six siblings, my parents and his two brothers, sister, and mom. It was a joyous occasion with Fulton and Archie wearing adorable matching seersucker suits and saddle shoes. Matilda and her sister Lauren had on stylish and fun Betsy Johnson dresses. Lauren was in her glory, bossing her little brother around and connecting with the adults. Matilda, on the other hand, was just miserable; we have the pictures to prove it. By that time, Matilda was an angry sixteen-year-old, already out of control. Lauren, age twelve, was agreeable to almost everything, and Archie, at barely seven, was just happy to have a daddy figure around. I knew they all needed some stability and not the kind I'd created trying to be both mother and father. I'd done the best job I could, but it was time to stop letting my own fears chart the course for our collective future. Just a month before my youngest sibling's beachside wedding, we were married at an old church down the street from my home with a small reception that included our closest friends and families. It was more than I could have asked for and although our best man (Archie), dropped our rings into the cuff of his pants and then crawled around on the floor trying to find them, the marriage stuck. It was an unbelievably hot day, but almost perfect for July. My very formal father, also in seersucker and a bow tie, kept watching Pastor Sam's feet during the entire service. Sam was wearing flip-flops. His response, "Franco! You told me this was casual." No Franco family event is ever really casual. My father would have given Frank Sinatra a run for his money in the style department.

Fulton tried—he tried hard—but my gut told me it would take a decade for Matilda to warm up to him. Sadly, I was just about dead-on with that prophecy. I had come a long way from the chaos and mayhem of my seventeen-year dysfunctional marriage. Fulton was stable, solid, and trustworthy. I felt confident that I'd done the right thing and felt just slightly superior that I was clearly winning in the second marriage category.

Through his role at the church, we began new adventures. Fulton was responsible for driving involvement for many community projects. A new head pastor, however, wanted to expand globally and so a trip to Nicaragua to explore partnership with an organization supporting multiple orphanages was set in motion. I had not been on a mission trip prior to this and was looking forward to it. As a child, we raised money for poor children throughout the world, but Catholics rarely went on mission trips. In fact, I'm not sure I knew what that even meant. I asked Matilda to go, hoping to bond with her and give her a global perspective on her own life and suffering. She seemed excited about it; I hoped that it might draw us closer.

I still remember the smell of mangos warming in the sun at the main orphanage outside of Managua where we were billeted. Nicaragua, once the breadbasket of Central America, was reduced to rubble and chaos. Children were begging in the streets of the capital; a beautiful Catholic church lay in ruin and miles of shacks with tin roofs stretched out in all directions from the city center. Matilda was so upset about the kids begging and blocking cars on a busy main thoroughfare. Just twenty minutes into our trip, she was reduced to tears. She had grown a hard shell, but inside was, and is, very tender hearted.

The leader of the organization we were partnered with kept us moving to several different orphanage locations, meeting the staff and spending time with the children on activities and Bible studies. Matilda easily fell in love with all the children we met, which wasn't difficult. She already had a teacher's heart and a deep well of discernment about wounding. At an orphanage high up in the mountains, in a relatively rural area, she realized how abused the kids were and how little treatment (if any) they would ever receive for that trauma. Basics like dental care were a luxury and although they were safe, fed, and educated, medical or emotional care was still modest if non-existent.

Her broken heart connected on a spiritual level with the caregivers and children.

In the latter part of our week, the organizer took us to what was to be the most difficult and yet amazing interaction of the entire trip. The destination was a massive garbage dump in the country's capital Managua—the home to more than 1,000 people, half of whom were children. It is the largest garbage dump in Central America and known as the "City of Trash." Reading that is incomprehensible to our American sensibilities; seeing it is an entirely different level of horror. Children play in squalor while their parents pick through garbage, harvesting tin and plastic for pennies. Babies are routinely run over by the endless parade of garbage trucks coming in and out of the dump. A Nicaraguan couple, moved by the spirit, left a middle-income lifestyle to start a daycare just outside the gates of the dump. Their mission was to save the children at risk, left alone while their mothers worked alongside their partners or as prostitutes. Yes, a prostitute in a garbage dump, perhaps the lowest socioeconomic level in any society. In spite of that proximity, the daycare was a sunny, happy place filled with noisy children running around and enjoying group activities. You could feel the joy and see it in the faces of the active one-, two-, three-, and four-year-old kids.

As soon as we walked in, a middle-aged woman made a beeline for Matilda, as if she knew her. She was clearly a leader and I watched her speak to my daughter from across the noisy room very intently. I noticed Matilda's face begin to crumble and her eyes well up. I was about to intervene when our guide leaned over to me and said, "She's a prophet." Again, my Catholic brain was like, what? Are there really prophets in this world and, if so, are they located near massive Central American garbage dumps? Eventually we were introduced to Maria, who came directly to me and put her arms around me with intensity and familiarity that seemed strange but not uncomfortable.

She shared that she was speaking to Matilda in Spanish, interesting because Matilda is small and very pale and doesn't look like the person you'd pick out as the translator in our group. She said to me in English, "I was telling your daughter that her life was going to have great meaning and it would help many, many others. I also told her you love her more than she will ever understand." We were both weeping at that point, but they were tears of joy. I had been so worried about the direction that Matilda's life was taking that it seemed farfetched she would survive let alone be an agent for good. We left that meeting and headed to the dump with our minds opened about what caring for others really meant and what real gratitude was about versus the materialistic version shared by many Americans.

At the end of our week, the leader told our group that if the children in the orphanages could learn English, they would be able to find good work that would pay far more than anything a college education would deliver—a remote possibility for most of them. Matilda piped up, "I could do that, Mom. I can teach them English." She was not yet seventeen, but the determination in her face made it clear this was not a random thought. She was serious. When we returned home, I reached out to the organization and told them I had a young adult who was interested in coming back to teach English. Surprisingly, they took us up on it and in the spring, she left for Managua alone, a small bag and laptop in hand. As we said goodbye in Atlanta, I was not the least bit nervous. I felt like this was exactly what she needed to do at just that moment. She spent almost nine months working between two orphanages. They took her up on her offer and she quickly became a full-time teacher covering much more than English. Matilda had learned Spanish from Nancy, the woman I hired to help me survive being a single mom. A nurse from Guatemala, Nancy was at Archie's daycare and came to us full-time when he was about two. Nancy spoke to all three children mostly in Spanish and took her role seriously. We called her "second mommy" because she really saved me in those single years when I was trying to keep it together. To this day, Nancy is part of all graduations, weddings, and events that matter in the kids' lives.

However, with a high school diploma and Guatemalan accent, Matilda was not exactly qualified for such a big role. However, she did it and did it with grace. It was there, alone among the mango trees, that she discovered her calling to teach. This would take on greater significance in college and afterward. It was the most difficult and most rewarding thing she had ever done. We are both grateful for the words of the prophet giving birth to her journey toward giving back to others.

I called Cricket to cancel her phone plan once she was ensconced in her new Central American home. Something told me to ask where the woman in the call center was located. She hesitated, wanting to keep up the "game" that this was an all-American company. She finally shared that she was in a call center in Managua, Nicaragua. I was floored as tears slid down my face. I told her about Matilda and why she was there. She said, "Don't worry, we'll take good care of her." I thanked God for this promise of protection delivered by a Cricket customer service person deep in the heart of Central America.

There was so much more life and suffering to experience—but God had a plan.

> We have not obeyed the Lord our God, for we have not followed the instructions he gave us through his servants the prophets. (Daniel 9:10 NLT)

Miracle 5

The Healing

After the end of my first marriage, and a four-year period spent as a single mom, I was once again a married woman. A man was living in our home and the children were banished from sleepovers in mom's queen-sized bed. That didn't go over well, especially with my oldest. My husband was married for twenty-three years to an artist, whose work hangs on our walls along with paintings created by my father and grandmother. I wanted Fulton to feel comfortable in the Victorian home I refused to leave in downtown Franklin. Therefore, into our lives he landed. To be fair, I did try to warn him about a life with three children, some of them surly.

I took him to my therapist to attempt to explain what things were going to be like dealing with a full-blown teenager, an almost teen, a slightly over-mommied little boy—and one very hostile ex-husband deep in the throes of addiction. He brushed off the warnings, convinced he had enough love for all of us and enough patience to deal with my ex.

God bless him, as we say in the south.

He also gave me the most generous gift I ever received. He erased the one significant financial stress I had left to bear— funding my children's college education. Without blinking an eye, he told me he wanted to take the equity from the house he lived in for eighteen years with his first wife and put that money into their college funds. I wept in relief and disbelief. We didn't sell his house right away. After our wedding, he moved in to my home and offered my sister, her husband, and their new baby his home, rent free, as her husband was in a job transition. Again, he was generous beyond belief. She used to joke that some of the furniture he gave them was "brought to you by a generous donation from the Fulton Thompson Foundation."

They moved out about a year later to relocate to a new job in Columbia, South Carolina and we then put the house on the market. Fulton had renovated it after his wife's passing and we knew it would go quickly. We sold it to a young couple; it was their first home together. Just three months later in 2010, a 1,000-year flood caused massive destruction, wiping out thousands of homes, including his. He didn't have flood insurance, and neither did the buyers. Thankfully the young couple had wealthy parents who helped them to rebuild— another miracle for both of us.

We had careers we loved: he was a pastor at a large church where people appreciated and respected him, and I was an executive in a five-hospital Catholic health system. We were operating at the "top of our license," so to speak, and it felt good. Our jobs were more than that—they felt like callings. We were right where we needed to be. Then, within just a few months, I lost my job and so did Fulton. It seemed impossible. We were both literally in shock. Nothing made sense and I called out to God for answers. There were none. I found another position quickly, as I had always had a bit of a side hustle going with consulting work. Fulton was not as lucky.

He was fifty-three, had diverse and amazing experience, but no one wanted to hire someone who spent the last decade as a pastor. He had built thirteen Habitat for Humanity houses during his tenure as a pastor and the local organization reached out about making him the chief executive. When it didn't happen, he was distraught. He never really looked for a job before. His career had many magical twists and turns, but opportunities just came to him without having to seek them out. In my world, that wasn't how life worked. I was very good at creating a resume and did that often for my friends and family. I made him a gorgeous resume and even reached out to my own network to help him kick-off the search for a new career.

The only upside to this season of life was that we were now free to remain at my church. He learned to love it there and we both acknowledged the spirit of God was most assuredly in the house. I felt terrible because I did not have that same feeling in his church. I felt the love the congregation had for him, but not the same tingling, Spirit-filled sensation so common at my home church. As a recovering Catholic, I was certainly no expert. I wondered at first if I was just feeling awkward and judged because their executive pastor married a divorcee ten years his junior with three kids. Insecure or not, no one put their hands in the air, and no one sang at the top of their lungs. It just wasn't the same. His life dramatically changed again, unmoored from a position he held for a decade, the last connection to his former life. The wave of grief from his wife's death that was suspended during our courtship and new marriage came roaring back and nearly drowned him.

As he withdrew, I begin to quietly, and then not so quietly, lose my mind.

How did a man who always worked, who took care of his wife to the bitter end, who had allowed her the luxury to focus on her art for years suddenly just stop working? Did I emasculate him? Was I being punished? After years of dealing with a depressed man who didn't help much, financially or otherwise, I just simply couldn't do it. I cried out to God, to my friends, to my church, and to my recovery family. This wasn't what I signed up for. I just couldn't take care of another able-bodied man. I had nothing left; my love tank was officially empty. I begin to feel that nagging existential anxiety I lived with for so long. I carefully filled a giant backpack up with rocks of regret, anger, expectation, and grief, hoisted it on my back and began to drag it around once again. It was crushing me. My husband had abandoned me (again), and God seemed far away.

Then he became sick—very sick.

In the fall of 2010, I was in San Francisco, California for a conference. A friend, and the company's chief financial officer, and I decided our husbands should join us for a long weekend after the event ended. They flew out together. Two older bald guys flying to San Francisco together was fairly humorous—until it wasn't. Her husband was a surgeon and, by the time they arrived at our hotel on Russian Hill, he told Fulton that when he got home, he needed to have his throat and lungs scoped. Fulton was coughing nonstop. What had started as allergies, or so we thought, escalated into something much more insidious. He was coughing up blood and every once in a while, a pebble-like material would fly out—it was extremely concerning. In spite of this, the weekend was fun for all of us. I was able to run across the Golden Gate Bridge and eat some amazing food, but the continuous coughing was straining all of us, especially Fulton.

Once back home, thanks to our friend, we went to a specialist at a large hospital in Nashville. The physician we met had an interesting name that in Italian meant "Fat Eater." I couldn't help but point that out because the man was about five feet six inches tall and couldn't have weighed more than 140 pounds. Surprised that I knew what his name meant in English, he shared that his grandfather was an immigrant, and he was very heavy, so the name may have been a nickname. Few in Nashville would have taken notice, and although this was a serious appointment, our casual banter helped to break the ice and build what I expected to be a long-term relationship—at least I hoped.

They took scans and set a date for an endoscopy to validate the diagnosis the doctor suspected. He was correct: Fulton had fibrosing mediastinitis, a condition affecting the area between the lungs (mediastinum) which contains the heart, large blood vessels, windpipe (trachea), esophagus, and lymph nodes. It is caused by bird flu (histoplasmosis), an illness that thousands of children across the southern United States get annually. However, for a rare portion of that population, the virus remains in the host and over decades creates rock-like growths around the lymph nodes that begin to cause issues later in adulthood. The doctor removed some of them with the scope but there was no medication-based treatment or surgery for this condition. The end game involves removing a lung. Even that would only buy time, as the risk is high that the condition would continue unabated to the other lung.

The physician showed us the images and said he was 100 percent certain of the diagnosis and the forecast. We would continue to check-in as the disease progressed but that was about all that could be done outside of steroids for the continual irritation. All I heard in the moment was, "Thank God, it's not cancer." That was enough to keep me relatively calm. I've always been a glass half-full person, prone to denial, but I knew Fulton was more in touch with the reality of the situation. He watched his first wife die. His focus and prayer became simply to show his new wife and kids how a Christian man handles himself when facing a death sentence. I was numb. I had been so angry because he was pouring himself into woodworking and hobbies and not looking for a job that this new crisis just didn't register fully. I couldn't help but feel defeated. Was this really what trusting God was all about: more suffering and more loss? Was my ingratitude being punished? How quickly I spiraled to what I viewed as shame-based thinking.

Externally, I kept my chin up and threw myself into work. To his credit, he maintained a good attitude. He was no longer depressed and grieving. We were both trying to live in the moment and praying daily for as much time as was God's will.

A few months later, our church decided to host a healing service. It was a Thursday evening, and I was unable to join him but was glad he was going. We saw miracles happen and it was important for both of us to ask for healing as we are called to ask God directly for all things. I wasn't holding out much hope, still believing that those sorts of giant, miraculous events were for other people. As he went forward that night, dear friends of ours met him at the altar with open arms. They are prayer warriors and have been directly involved in healings with other church members and people around the world. He didn't ask for a cure, he asked for the strength to die well. We believe in heaven and full healing on the other side of the veil. Certainly, we hope to live long lives, but we also know we are promised death is not the end. It was very brave. He came home that night upbeat and we had a good evening but then went back to our lives.

One morning, not long after, I woke up to silence. He was not coughing.

At first, it was very noticeable. Months and months of deep, brutal coughing had become the norm, but then all of a sudden, it was quiet. He had a regular appointment with Dr. Mangialardi a week or so later, and we went together, nervous to say much of anything. He once again did a chest CT scan and while we waited in the small, sterile room, we were nearly giddy with anticipation. We both felt like he was better, but cured—that was not clear. I wasn't even sure a scan would show anything. As the doctor opened the door, a slight smile spread across his face. He shared he almost never had good news for anyone in this clinic, but he had very good news for us. He laid out the former scans to show us what was obviously the disease and then the new scans of what appeared to be normal lungs. I almost said, "Whose are those?" The doctor pressed forward, frantically making the point over and over that Fulton did have this disease and now he did not. Fulton smiled broadly, his eyes twinkling. He said, "Well Dr. Mangialardi, I guess this is a miracle." There was a moment of silence as we all let that sink in.

I don't know why Fulton received a miracle when so many others don't. I suppose we won't know that until we are with Jesus face to face and all questions are answered. Now it was time to thank God for this amazing gift, and for loving us enough to give us more time to find our way back to each other.

> O LORD my God, I cried to you for help, and you
> restored my health. (Psalm 30:2)

Miracle 6

Fear and Marriage, Part 2: "Will you trust me now?"

Then we all lived happily ever after.

Well, not exactly.

When I give my testimony, I often use that statement to break my life into stories. It's become a joke in our family. I wanted so badly for that to be real, for the white knight to pick me up and ride us off into the sunset, but alas, that is fantasy. Life is not a Disney princess movie. The reality of our existence in a broken world more closely resembles an obstacle course full of very difficult events, people, and experiences. I'm not sure I was ever told that; in fact, I was told the opposite. In my family of origin, if you studied enough, loved deeply enough, and worked harder than everyone else, you were bound to succeed. However, my own life had not born that out and acknowledging reality was devastating. This was another reminder that I was not in control.

In my obstacle course-filled life, once I got over the giant wall and mud pit, there was another challenge right around the corner. I've learned in recovery that the goal isn't to avoid difficult things. Rather, the goal is to flow with them, accepting life on life's terms. That only took me about fifty years to master. If I'm honest, I have to work on that every single day. The exercise metaphor works in this case. To create muscle memory, to stay in the moment, to remain spiritually grounded and not live for tomorrow or dwell on the past requires regular, ongoing exercise.

Fulton was healed, but our marriage was not. I was the primary breadwinner, and he was still indulging obsessively in his new hobby. My husband is a man on a mission in all things. When he decides to do something, it is 1000 percent all-consuming until it is perfected. I must admit I take the opposite approach to life. I'm about consistency and remaining steady in a chaotic world. Every week, when Fulton asks me if I'm going running, I repeat, "What day is it?" For more than twenty-two years, I have run Monday, Wednesday, and Saturday with my neighbor and dear friend. She's a tiny, FBI agent who never fails to show up and has kept me compliant to a routine that I love. We also talk nonstop about every aspect of our lives, the good and the bad.

I could have the rest of time and never perfect any of the things he has taught himself to do. We often joke that apparently, this is another opportunity for the eHarmony algorithm. One day I will reach out to Dr. Warren and share my suggestions. I'm going to add that data point as well as a level of neatness scale, and why not throw in love languages while we're at it?

Looking back, I can see that my gratitude waned over the next few years. Fulton became a highly skilled wood turner (wooden bowl maker), and I became increasingly angry and frustrated. I was once again taking care of a now healthy husband and my children. If I was being honest, I was mentally and spiritually worn out. Looking back, we never had a conversation about next steps after his career as a pastor came to an end. I wanted him to find something he loved but also something that would contribute to the family. We had not made an agreement that I would work, and he would retire. I didn't want much; I knew I would be the anchor provider, but I wasn't willing to be the only provider. I complained to everyone: siblings, my pastor's wife, my small group, my running buddy, and finally my husband. Although I didn't stuff my feelings this time, not much changed and we moved quietly and awkwardly forward. During that time, a few new friends came into our life. One couple had been involved in a non-profit with me and were also very involved in Fulton's former church. We had also recently met an elderly businessman who was a recent widower experiencing what Fulton had just lived through a few years prior. Like most relationships, these began with the best of intentions but devolved overtime into an unhealthy form of emotional support for me as well as the source of a busy social life for us.

We were busy, but not happy.

I was invested in not spending much time alone with my husband to avoid having the same discussion over and over. I wanted to manage the situation on my own. I had cried out to God and felt He was not listening to me. I took power back and was determined to ride the line of relying on emotional support from men who were not my husband. I heard over the years that men and women couldn't really be friends. I didn't agree with that—I had been in corporate America for twenty years at that point and fought for my place in a man's world. There had never been many options for female mentors, so I had positioned myself as "one of the boys"—an equal and a peer. Like most women, I had not slowed down enough to invest in female networking. There were not many women in my position early on, and later I just simply didn't have the time. In that season, I justified these male relationships as mentors I needed to continue moving up the corporate ladder. I was lonely, needing a massive amount of validation and support. I had heard after moving to Nashville that there were men who would not even have a business lunch with a woman alone. I found that to be very old-fashioned and almost offensive.

I don't feel that way any longer.

The truth is there is real danger leaning on a man who is not your husband. As women, we bond emotionally. When a man listens, supports our careers, takes our side, and even offers protection (physically or emotionally), it's deeply moving and creates attachment. The line that is crossed is often opening up about issues in your own marriage—it's a boundary that signals you are raw and vulnerable. I was wounded. I couldn't bear taking care of another husband. I couldn't stand being lonely in my own home and in another marriage. I wasn't working my recovery program and I certainly didn't have healthy boundaries in place.

I traveled to Boston with one of our new friends, the recent widower, for a medical conference. I was looking for some healthy networking and this seemed like a good opportunity. However, things were odd and uncomfortable, and I ended up hiding in my room most of the time to stay away from him. My husband didn't react when I shared my discomfort; he seemed lost in his own world, which wasn't intersecting with mine.

Not long after, we went to the beach with another couple who had become close friends. They had been together forever and shared our belief system. They were successful and owned a beautiful home on the coast. They had quickly become our best friends and the never-ending social events were always entertaining. I'm a social butterfly and I loved it. I didn't have to plan anything because they always had something exciting going on. What could go wrong?

One day, heading home from my office in a small convertible with the top down, I was listening to music when I noticed guys in a truck next to me were whistling and trying to get my attention. It was unnerving but easy to ignore. As I sat there trying not look to my left, I got a text message which said, "I have my finger on the trigger." Our friend was on the other side of the truck, quietly watching the show from his own vehicle. A gun advocate, he always carried a weapon and knew how to use it. A smile crossed my face. I couldn't help but be impressed and feel safe under the protective gaze of this successful man. I was now viewing him as a protector, a role that should have been taken by my husband.

Danger, danger, danger.

The beach has always been a spiritual place for me. It reminds us that we are small, and the world is large. The ocean is peaceful, vast, and unstoppable. I love to run on the beach, preferably barefoot and alone. Running has long been therapeutic; it is the only time I think only of my breath and what is right in front of me. During this particular trip, I was also running away from the dangerous dance I found myself engaged in, riding the line between appropriate and inappropriate, safety and risk, comfort and loneliness. The truth is I was no longer letting God lead me, and I was done hoping to have a husband who would act as a leader in my family. I literally had conscious thoughts that went something like this: *Well if you won't give me what I want, then I'll take care of it myself.* I knew better after years of consistent time invested in Al-Anon working hard on my codependence, but like so many others, I figured I no longer needed it as I had successfully moved on and married up.

It's amazing how quickly we fall back into bad habits, and what desperation will do to carefully constructed boundaries. I knew I was walking on very thin ice; and there seemed to be no hope for change. I'd been crying out for so long that giving up seemed reasonable. I wanted to feel as if someone cared, and I desperately needed to hear that my work efforts were at least appreciated.

I took off for a run, alone, in the beautiful sunshine of a Saturday morning. I was about a mile into the run, my heart and breathing calm with the ocean breeze in my face. There was literally no one but me on the beach; it was quiet as I ran in and out of the edge of the surf line. Out of nowhere, I heard a voice, loud and clear as a bell, say, "Will you trust me now?" I literally spun around looking for the source. It was clear to me that whoever had spoken, the message was for me. I didn't doubt that, but there was no one within a half-mile of where I found myself. I fell on my knees and cried. I was trying so hard to trust but I was once again failing. I wish I could say that I immediately repented, turning away from the forbidden fruit. The truth is, the flesh is weak, and I soon discovered that under the right set of circumstances, we are all capable of sin. I had put myself on such a martyr's perch during my first marriage, judging the failure of mere mortals harshly. However, even after several years of recovery work in Al-Anon, I realized my Achilles heel: love addiction.

It took time, repentance, and some difficult conversations to establish healthy boundaries, but eventually, through a tremendous work of grace, God intervened and softened my heart and my husband's. We cleaned up our lives, pushed all our faux friends out and recommitted to moving forward together. Humility and repentance had given me a totally new perspective. The martyr was gone, and I joined the ranks of failed human beings. It was honestly a relief to know that I was not bound for sainthood. Humility creates empathy and I'm pleased to say that this experience, although difficult and painful, has made me into a much kinder person, even kinder to myself. I didn't have to be perfect to deserve love. I was lovable in my brokenness and so was he.

Fulton finally agreed to train under a friend of ours who owned a residential window cleaning company. Fifty-plus-year old former pastors with backgrounds in TV and engineering were not highly sought at that time. He was not comfortable with self-promotion. But having transitioned between industries years prior, I had a vast network and had figured out how to always be working. The side hustle was my go-to move so that if Plan A failed, there was always Plan B.

As humbling as it was, like everything he chooses to do, he poured himself into learning the business and launching his own. Fulton's window cleaning company grew to a solid base of great clients and enough work and income to keep him busy and me peaceful. I will say that once Fulton and his team of slightly older than middle-aged church guys jelled into a cohesive unit, they ministered to people all over our county. I still hear stories about how they would pray with clients or their children over a wide variety of issues. That experience showed us both that we can work for Jesus in nearly any calling if we just listen to His direction.

Having him once again gainfully employed reduced much of my distress and gave him purpose. We still had things to work on, but the entire episode made it clear to me that God of the universe never gives up on us. He chases us down and speaks to us in a manner we can hear when we are ready. He is bigger than our fears, our wounds, and our sadness. We can't see the long view, but He can. I doubted our marriage, but He did not. Today I can say I trust Him, and my husband has taken the role of spiritual leader. Marriage is never easy.

It takes work and commitment, and that commitment must be made daily.

We still have work to do, but after launching Celebrate Recovery (a Christian twelve-step program) at our church, we both made another commitment to stay in recovery, working our programs and guiding others through the process. This has been instrumental in finding our way back to trusting one another. We still have communication problems, but we are not running away from those issues or our marriage. Rather, we are both focused on pursuing our relationships with God with as much passion as we do other things in our lives that don't have the weight of eternal value.

> See, God has come to save me. I will trust in him and not be afraid. The LORD GOD is my strength and my song; he has given me victory. (Isaiah 12:2 NLT)

Miracle 7

The Josiah Story (and the Stranger on the Mountain)

After moving through her chaotic teens, my oldest seemed to be on a very positive trajectory. Her experience in Nicaragua had changed her life and mine in many ways. I was so hopeful she would veer from the path set by her father and follow the path her eternal Father had planned for her life. She returned home from the third world and headed off to college in Chattanooga, Tennessee. The University of Tennessee Chattanooga is a beautiful campus with the feel of a private college. The minute she walked into the language school, she knew she was home. We were greeted by a French professor who Matilda took a shine to immediately. I believe the feeling was mutual. Her thirst for knowledge and academic validation was something we had in common, and I felt like I was leaving her in safe place.

Sadly, I was wrong.

Although her grades never dipped, she dove headfirst into the insanity of college life, including a never-ending supply of parties fueled by a thirst for alcohol and drugs. I had trained her well—succeed in school and nothing else matters—something that was passed down to me, but hopefully ends with this generation. She had eighteen credits from her efforts in high school because she was dual enrolled at a local community college. As a result, her freshman year was really a sophomore year. This was another academic achievement that masked the deep pain, anger, and wounding she felt inside. The train was coming down the tracks and I had no idea; neither did she. She turned twenty in July and in September, headed back to Chattanooga for her second year. At that time, she was dating a boy from our hometown who seemed blessedly "normal." I let myself believe that finally she was moving in the right direction.

I felt hopeful as the trees began to change colors and my forty-sixth birthday loomed ahead. On a sunny Sunday morning, we packed Archie, Lauren, Fulton, and myself into the car to head to church. A strange number from Chattanooga popped up on my phone. I decided to answer it as something in my spirit told me this was important. The nurse on the other end was from Erlanger Hospital. My heart stopped. She spoke quickly and efficiently. A Jane Doe had been brought in early that morning and was just identified as my daughter. She was in a coma and "decisions needed to be made." We were instructed to get there as soon as possible. I literally went numb as a chill when through my body. Is this it? Am I going to have the strength to accept whatever happens and still continue on?

Just two years prior, my pastor's oldest child, a young man named Jacob, had gone to heaven due to a very random car accident. I was with them in the hospital along with several hundred prayer warriors from our church. I was there when they made the decision to let him go and honor his wish to be an organ donor, a decision he had made just a few months prior. Their grace in that situation came to mind as I tried to simply breathe. In my fervent and quiet prayers, I began to ask Jacob to take his army of angels to surround her bed in the hospital and protect her. It felt natural and meaningful.

I called my pastor, who answered on the first ring, even though he was in between sermons. At "Franco, what's up?" I burst into tears. I felt terrible dumping this on him and his sweet wife, who were still grieving. I knew they would be there for me, and I needed their experience, strength, and hope. He said he would be with us praying every step of the way as our car headed down I-24 as quickly as possible. We arrived at Erlanger and walked into the emergency department, desperate for information. The boyfriend was there and clearly out of his mind, still tripping from the drugs they had been taking as the sun had risen that morning. My husband made a beeline for him, and I'm pretty sure threatened his life—not that he could even hear it or focus properly at that moment. When we were able to see her after thirty minutes or so, she was on a ventilator, filthy with leaves and twigs all through her hair. Her pretty face was now deathly pale. I still had not gotten any feedback on what happened, but over the next few hours the story came together.

After a night of partying, she and several of her friends had gotten up early to head to a mountaintop outside of Chattanooga called Stringer's Ridge to watch the sun rise. After dropping (ingesting) acid, it became clear something was wrong. Matilda began to seize and fell forward down a ravine about 150 feet below a guardrail she was sitting on. Terrified but incapable of thought beyond the fact that they didn't want to get in trouble, the others did nothing. It's an interesting thing about drug use: it literally removes all self-control. That loss of self and sense includes any empathy for anyone else. In so many ways, the soul is suspended, trapped, and unable to function as the body is given to wickedness in the name of escape. It wasn't that the boyfriend didn't care; he literally couldn't care. Of course, that was of no interest to Fulton, who wanted to take him outside and beat him to death, blaming this kid for the decisions made by our daughter.

Good friends left Nashville, picked up clothes and other essentials for me, and came to our aid. That's what healthy friends do in a crisis. Matilda's real friends dropped everything to come be by her side, from as far as California. I don't remember much other than the continual outreach from family and friends who stood with us, including my older sister, who also jumped in a car and drove non-stop from West Virginia. My big sis came with me to Matilda's apartment to help get some of her things together, with hopeful anticipation that she would wake up and leave the hospital. Her small apartment looked like a bomb had gone off. This was no real surprise, but the physical manifestation of the chaos in her life broke my heart and flew in the face of the excellent grades and positive feedback from professors. This was the great schism in her young life.

A friend also named Jacob had come down from Nashville. We knew this young man well and knew he loved her dearly. We spent time talking, crying, and sharing Matilda stories. It was a great distraction. One of my best friends literally picked all the leaves and debris out of her hair while another brought down Manhattan mixings. It was a loving but difficult time; I was blessed with support from those closest to us who were there for every minute. As the hours passed, we began to put the pieces together around what happened after she tumbled down the mountain. Apparently, a lone hiker at 6:00 a.m. on a Sunday came upon her and called for help. This mystery woman was never identified, not by the EMTs, the police, or by Matilda's friends. Had it not been for her action, it is clear Matilda would have died in that ravine. I owe this guardian angel a debt of gratitude. Another miracle to add to the official record.

My pastor checked in regularly, suffering with me from a place of deep understanding. Then, on the third day (literally), she woke up. I was frantic as questions around brain damage could not be ascertained until she was alert, but the minute she opened her mouth, the smart-alecky Matilda was clearly 100 percent intact. One of the first things she shared was that she had been speaking to Jacob. I, of course, thought she meant the Jacob who was with us at Erlanger in the flesh. However, she quickly corrected me and said, "No, Jacob Bauman." I started to tear up and immediately reached out to Sam and Heather, who cried with me. An army of angels had indeed come to her aid, and we would speak of this over the years as just another example of God's mercy and favor. I don't know why one young person goes to heaven and another remains on this earth. I half-jokingly told Matilda that clearly God had more for her to work out, more to learn, more to do. I yearn for the day when we know the answers to those questions.

After she was discharged from the hospital, I brought her home for the rest of the semester. She had suffered brain damage in the form of significant short-term memory loss, her speech was impacted, and she would be diagnosed with epilepsy. In addition to all of that, she was also having mobility issues. The insurance company rejected the recommendation of four different neurologists for in-patient therapy, so we began a long process of occupational therapy, physical therapy, and speech therapy in outpatient settings. These concluded a few months later in a neuro-psych assessment given by a psychologist at Vanderbilt. It was in the same office shared by an MD PhD brain surgeon who had become a dear friend over some international travel to Saudi Arabia and in the days before Jacob went to heaven. Dr. Kaplan was there and saw Jacob in the ER as he was brought in that evening. I'm always amazed at the layers of my life that overlap in profound ways. The psychologist had that Sigmund Freud look: he was quiet with thoughtful eyes and a dark, neatly trimmed beard. When we started the assessment and he heard about the accident and brain damage, I sensed he expected her to be in much worse condition. The testing would reveal the truth one way or another and set a new starting point for Matilda's life. Would she be ready to go back to school, and if not, what did the future look like for her? Would she ever be back to 100 percent? As we waited for the results, I had to admit I was more concerned than she seemed to be. Matilda loves tests and was delighted to see where she was in terms of cognitive ability. As we sat in his small office, in a low calm voice, the good doctor looked at her with great intensity and said, "If you just stay sober, you can do anything you want with your life."

That was a moment. She heard him and acknowledged what he said. I had hope at that point she was going to be able to fulfill the destiny prophesied over her in Nicaragua, but only time would tell.

> For he will order his angels to protect you wherever you go. They will hold you up with their hands so you won't even hurt your foot on a stone. (Psalm 91:11–12 NLT)

Miracle 8

The Holy Spirit Seat Belt

By the time Matilda arrived at her senior year in college, she made peace with her sobriety and was dedicated to having her senior thesis published as an undergrad. She seemed to be very connected to recovery, where she found a tremendous lifeline and support group of people who understood her. Two years prior, I told her I was not going to clean her up again, a promise that would require the love and support of my Al-Anon home group to keep. My codependent nature of wanting to save everyone I loved would not help her lead a life free of drugs and alcohol. Although some family members wondered why I would send her back to the "scene of the crime," I prayed about it and knew it was her life to live. She had what she needed to finish what she started there. It took all I had not to think about what she was doing (or not doing) but I "let go and let God." She told me she would seek recovery and agreed to attend meetings. I would, of course, have no way of knowing if she was going, but it was out of my hands. She told me later that there were times she really wanted to use, and in fact, intended to use, but felt like she needed at the very least go to a meeting to check the box. She walked into her first meeting believing it to be AA (Alcoholics Anonymous). It was not; it was an NA (Narcotics Anonymous) meeting and a business meeting at that. Business meetings are generally to make decisions about how the group functions, so they are not meetings for newcomers. For whatever reason she stayed, and she found a family who understood her. She remains as engaged today as she was in that first meeting nearly ten years ago. I thank God every night for another day clean.

In addition, her passion for the immigrant Hispanic community led her to internships helping Spanish-speaking people communicate effectively in medical appointments in Chattanooga. She also found an internship working with inner city middle and high school students. In that role, she discovered she had a natural talent for teaching and dealing with kids from chaotic urban backgrounds. She had the right amount of edge to be authentic with them and enough discernment to see through their rough exteriors to skills hidden under layers of abuse and neglect. One of her students came to school in dirty clothes, had a messy backpack, and was nearly always uncommunicative. Within a week, she figured out that this young man was not unintelligent, as she'd been told. He was certainly not being cared for or parented, but he had insight. She went to her program director and shared her thoughts about his potential. Low and behold, they shepherded him into some testing and discovered that he was in fact quite bright. That sort of personal insight is a literal gift from God. You can't learn it and I know it was a gift bestowed on my oldest child by the creator of the universe.

She continued to teach and moved on with a class of middle schoolers to high school in the same program. For her ninth-grade class, she was positioned as an assistant to a first-year teacher I referred to as the "the Dugger girl." Matilda was the polar opposite of this gal, and the kids didn't trust or respect the young teacher. It was certainly a daily battle between her and her teacher and the children due to different styles and levels of experience, empathy, and understanding. However, I think the experience taught them both a few things. In some strange way, her now obvious mobility issues garnered many comments from the students. There was no filter. "Why you walk funny?" was not uncommon. She met those kids without fear, and they came to respect her as another struggling person who understood not fitting in or having an easy life.

One rainy morning, at about 6:30 a.m., I was getting ready to fly back from a conference in St. Louis when I received a call from the 423 area code. Oh God, Chattanooga, here we go again. Something in my spirit told me to answer and not let this call roll to voicemail. It was an older man with a very country accent who knew my name. My heart stopped once I confirmed he had the right person. This kind, older gentleman shared that my daughter had been in a terrible car accident and things did not look very good, but she was speaking and asked him to call me. The EMTs were at the scene of the crash and deploying the jaws of life to extricate her from the older boxy Volvo we had bought as her college car. With little clarity about her status or what happened, I knew only one thing. I had to get home immediately and then travel the two hours to Chattanooga. With tears streaming down my face, I left the hotel and headed to the airport. I had to fly through Chicago and was sitting next to a pilot who was being ferried to a flight out of Midway. By the time we were in the air leaving St. Louis, I had received a link to a news story from my middle child, who was in high school back in Franklin. She had left Franklin with her father to head to Chattanooga. The news story did nothing to provide comfort. The scene was horrific, the entire roof of the dark green S70 was torn off, and it looked like a giant machine had crushed the front and back end into the center, forming a metal box. How could she have survived? I knew she was alive and that she was heading into surgery, but not much else. The pilot watched me re-watching the news link and figured out what was going on. The minute we landed in Illinois, he made sure I got off the plane first, walked me to my next flight, and even brought me coffee. The kindness of a stranger was nearly overwhelming. I believe I became a life-long member of the "biggest fans of Southwest Airlines" in that moment.

Landing in Nashville, I didn't even stop at our home but frantically headed down highway 24, hurtling toward the now familiar Erlanger hospital, praying for her life to be spared yet again. By the time I arrived, a group of friends from her NA home group were already congregating in the waiting room. I was given a quick update. She was just coming out of surgery. Her arm that had been crushed was now being held together by a metal plate, but miraculously she suffered no other significant damage. If you could see the car, it really was hard to believe. A photo of the destroyed vehicle made it on the Official Volvo Facebook "Survivor" page. They sent her a coffee mug and some other tchotchkes after we shared the image—a small consolation prize. That old car had a massive frame and air bag that saved her life. I recommend these cars for new drivers as they really are tanks.

In the recovery room post op, I asked the anesthesiologist about a new form of pain management: a pain ball that is generally used for knee and hip replacements. The anesthesiologist seemed surprised I knew about that option. Matilda had been honest with them when she was taken to the hospital. She said she was an addict and had to be very careful with any sort of narcotic. Yet it was not considered until I brought it up. I was told that wasn't protocol. Needless to say, twenty minutes later, they were setting her up with what amounts to an epidural for the arm. She could not feel anything and was not internalizing a dangerous drug that could potentially destroy her sobriety. I had learned about On-Q through a client relationship and had even interviewed patients who had major orthopedic procedures with narcotics and with On-Q. Sixty-five-year-old women who had both ankles rebuilt told me that, with the narcotics, by week six she was still in pain and was having suicidal thoughts. She had no history of substance use disorder (SUD) or even addictive behavior. With her second procedure, she had the On-Q system and never felt pain. Within a week, she was getting back to her life. It was shocking. Certainly, we can do better in our health system to train clinicians about substance use disorder and find creative strategies to protect people from the risk of relapse. After a few days in the hospital, I once again bundled my baby up and took her back home to heal.

On the drive home, we were both nervous. She was having PTSD and her pain level in other areas of her body from the trauma made sitting in the car miserable. To distract her, I asked her about that morning and what she remembered.

She shared the dramatic details and again I felt God's love warm me from head to toe. She was sitting at a stop light, ten cars back, as rain drizzled from a cold sky. She didn't have her seatbelt on, even though I continually harped on her about it literally since she had received her permit. She was not a compliant young adult. She said she then had a massive sense of dread, sitting there listening to her windshield wipers swish back and forth. Like a wave, it came over her and she reflexively gripped her seat belt. She had just clicked it into place when she looked in the rear-view mirror and saw a car barreling toward her, moving far too fast to stop in time. A woman, likely on her phone, hit her from behind so hard that her car, still at a dead stop, was forcibly shoved into oncoming traffic. She had no time to react and in horror saw the Budweiser beer truck heading directly for her, initiating a horrific head-on crash. The poor driver could do nothing to stop the inevitable. The impact sent one of his front wheels flying off and over her hood. That alone should have killed her that morning, but the tire somehow missed the front windshield by inches. The driver was able to get out of the truck and rushed to try to help. The woman who hit her from behind did not. She just sat there in her car until the police arrived.

The first responders were on site within minutes and although she was alert and conscious, they warned her that her legs were likely crushed. Worse, she could tell from their pained expressions they were not certain what would happen when they began to cut her out of the car. The entire engine and dashboard were pressing down on her lap. Matilda told them her legs were not crushed and was insistent she could move them. The EMTs were shocked to see what she had sensed was true. Once she was freed, it was clear that outside of her poor arm, she was in pretty good shape. Relief flooded through both she and her rescuers.

As she recovered at home, her students, many of whom still connect with her to this day on social media, reached out, concerned about her safety. Children who seemed to have so little in common with this small, very white teaching assistant had built a bond in the most human context based on shared suffering.

Another real miracle was a holy warning whispered in the ear of my child right before a horrific crash. Again, I have no idea why, but we have joked over the years that although the world keeps trying to kill her, God simply has other plans.

> Put on all of God's armor so that you will be able to stand firm against all strategies of the devil. (Ephesians 6:11 NLT)

Miracle 9

The Big Payback and Diagnosis

Once Matilda was able to head back to school, after recovering successfully from surgery (narcotic free), she returned to her small apartment. It was near the university, and I assumed a safe neighborhood. However, one evening while she was out at a meeting, someone broke in and stole her computer. She had been working feverishly on a senior thesis her favorite professor had been championing, with the objective of having it published while she was an undergrad. For someone with a brain injury, we all agreed that would be a lofty goal. The topic was a literary review of the book *One Hundred Years of Solitude* and her paper, all seventy pages, had to be written in Spanish. She had just sent the latest version to herself by email, ensuring that a copy was in the middle world of the internet, safe and removed from her hard drive. She was heartbroken, as it had taken so much to simply get back to school let alone focus on her passion for Central American literature. She called me in tears, but I calmly told her that it was just a computer, and we could replace it. I sent her to Best Buy to get another once she was certain the draft was safe.

She went to Best Buy and worked with a salesperson to find something functional and affordable. She got in line to pay, planning to immediately get back to work. Just as she was about to hand a credit card to the person at the register, a man's arm reached out from behind her and swiped his card instead. He calmly said, "I think I'm supposed to do that" and then he turned and walked out of the store. The clerk was of course shocked and asked her if she knew who he was: she did not. It was nearly $1,200—a large amount for a college kid and a gift from beyond this world given by an obedient, complete stranger. She called me with total wide-eyed surprise, saying, "Mom, you will never believe what happened!" We both laughed at the incredible favor and the God nod that what was stolen was replaced.

With her new computer, she finalized her thesis, and it was indeed published. By the time she was asked to defend it at a conference in Spokane, Washington, another challenge would begin to define her young life. She had mobility issues we were aware of since high school and that we assumed were related to the major spinal surgery to repair her malignant scoliosis when she was thirteen. A friend studying physical therapy asked if she'd participate in a project. By the end of it, he told her something was wrong, and she seemed to be getting worse. I remember not believing or wanting to believe feedback from a student.

My younger child Lauren, snuggled in between her brother and sister by just four and five years respectively, had been a fun, social child, and quite an athlete. She played soccer, she ran cross country, and in middle school, wanted to try her hand at volleyball. I played college basketball but had played volleyball in high school as well and really enjoyed watching the kids play any sport. For the first time, things just didn't click. While she made the team, she just didn't seem to catch on and wasn't playing much. By the time she began ninth grade, her interest in sports had waned and, not wanting to nag her, I let it go. One day she asked in a serious voice, "Mom, why didn't you teach me to swim?"

She shared that a friend was trying to help her learn to swim and it was very frustrating. I looked at her surprised and related that not only did she take swim lessons, but she'd been on a team in grade school at a local club we joined. I wrote this memory lapse off as the ongoing complaints of my middle child, who never seemed to get enough of my time or attention. I wrote a bunch of things off in that season which I'll always regret. As she neared her senior year in high school, she was working at a coffee shop with a large staircase and tables on both the first and second floors. One day, she fell on the stairs and was summarily fired. I began to believe she had an inner ear issue and even took her to the assessment organization called Brain Balance, a franchise that attempts to identify learning issues. Lauren insisted she had ADD and was having trouble focusing. A young gal barely out of college administered a series of assessments, both physical and academic, and concluded something was indeed wrong, but she didn't know what. She said it seemed to be impacting her balance. I was furious and likely not very nice as she shared her findings with us. I would later make amends to this young woman when the truth became clear. I will make life amends to my daughter until I leave this earth.

The issues persisted. Lauren would not wear heels or sandals and was struggling to walk up the stairs at high school. To make matters worse, her school was accusing her of being drunk and would not allow her to use the elevator. I booked an appointment at an ear, nose, and throat doctor to rule out some sort of inner ear issue. I wasn't able to join her, again believing that she was fine. The doctor told her that her ears were not an issue, and he thought it was some sort of neurologic issue. We booked an appointment with a neurologist here in Franklin, but I'm ashamed to say I was not able to attend that one either. He did a painful nerve conductivity test and told her he had a hunch as to what was wrong. After several years of not being heard, she was thrilled just to have someone acknowledge what she already understood in a deep place. Fulton and I joined Lauren a week or so later for the follow-up appointment, I was still 100 percent fighting against the belief that there was something significantly wrong. My codependence was getting the best of me. I wanted to believe so badly that everything was okay that I was willing to discount all the evidence. As we entered his office, Lauren was sitting on the exam table, the doctor was holding her big toe, and telling her to look away. A resident was watching closely as he moved her toe up and down and asked her if it was up or down. When she couldn't tell, he seemed nearly gleeful. I have said that it was his "Dr. House" moment. He explained that she had advanced neuropathy, and this was most certainly a genetic neurologic issue that was likely to continue to get worse.

And then he said, "Does anyone else in the family have similar issues?"

In a single moment, the truth shot through me like a bolt of lightning. Matilda. After denying all of this for so long, the truth was now unavoidable. I felt like I had fallen into a giant bottomless pit. Lauren, however, was so thrilled to be validated that she was nearly jubilant. I was terrified but tried to keep my thoughts and feelings to myself. I did what any Italian might do, and I narrowed my fear and concern into a focused rage, targeting this young physician and his callous behavior in sharing devastating news. I also immediately went into action mode. I knew the leading neurologist at Vanderbilt in Nashville. I reached out, and he directed me to another expert who oversaw the Movement Disorder Clinic. Due to my relationship with Dr. Kaufman, we were able to get an appointment to do genetic testing to figure out what was going on. Matilda had her hands full and, prior to knowing definitively, I didn't want to add to her burden. Staying sober and finishing college with a flourish was enough.

When the results came back, Lauren asked that her father and I join her to speak the doctor. I must admit I was not thrilled. We were in a year-long legal battle with him over my desire to send my son to a private Christian middle and high school. I knew it was the right thing to do for him, so we pushed through, but it was ugly, painful, and hurtful. Despite the discomfort of having my ex join us, I had no right at that point to complain. There we were, waiting on the good doctor to tell us something that would change our lives forever. Dr. Peters is a kind, calm man. He sat down and spoke to us all at eye level. He calmly explained that Lauren, and by default Matilda, had a form of muscular dystrophy called Friedrich's Ataxia. There is no cure, it is progressive, and both of them had the same defect score, roughly 600 on a scale of zero to 1,600. It is a genetic disorder, and their father and I were carriers of this defect. The chance of us meeting and having children was shockingly rare. The likelihood of us having a child with FA was one in four. Out of three children, he made it clear that our two girls were already affected by FA. I couldn't breathe, and I also couldn't react. This was not my moment. Lauren was still calm, pleased to be heard and know what this thing as was called. The good doctor was not hopeless and told us there was ongoing research and a cure was imminent.

It was my job to call Matilda and tell her what we now knew. She cried, and I cried. There would be many moments in the shower where my raw animal wail would be stifled by the fan and sound of hot water rushing to the floor. I cried out to God to change this, to heal them, to not take my daughters through the rest of their lives with this horrible disease. There were so many nights asking why, why, why.

Yet as I heard from so many others who suffer great tragedy, why not us?

The world is broken, and we are not guaranteed a smooth ride through this life. After everything we already survived, this new horror was just simply overwhelming. The worst of it was that there was nothing we could do. After all the money that Jerry Lewis and his telethons raised, there was still not a single treatment, much less a cure for any of the thirty different types of muscular dystrophy. After the loss of my first marriage, the life I originally hoped for, and a sense that the world was safe, I found myself utterly broken. However, I did my best not to show that to my children, who needed me to be strong.

In a moment of prayer a few years after the diagnosis, I distinctly heard a voice say, "I've already healed them." I knew that this meant spiritually. Their eternal health is of course more important than the brief period of time we spend on this planet. Whether they are healed in this life or the next, I will believe that His promises are true. The timing of course is not.

> Your promise revives me; it comforts me in all
> my troubles. (Psalm 119:50 NLT)

Miracle 10

A Bread Sacrifice

As a former Roman Catholic, I must admit that the book of Leviticus was not something I was very familiar with growing up. To this day, reading through it with any understanding or discernment is still a struggle. My husband, however, loves it when God speaks to him through random verses. One day during his Bible study, sitting quietly in our front living room, he opened the book to this chapter.

> "Anyone who cannot afford a lamb is to bring two doves or two young pigeons to the Lord as a penalty for their sin—one for a sin offering and the other for a burnt offering. They are to bring them to the priest, who shall first offer the one for the sin offering. He is to wring its head from its neck, not dividing it completely, and is to splash some of the blood of the sin offering against the side of the altar; the rest of the blood must be drained out at the base of the altar. It is a sin offering. The priest shall then offer the

other as a burnt offering in the prescribed way and make atonement for them for the sin they have committed, and they will be forgiven.

"If, however, they cannot afford two doves or two young pigeons, they are to bring as an offering for their sin a tenth of an ephah of the finest flour for a sin offering. They must not put olive oil or incense on it, because it is a sin offering. They are to bring it to the priest, who shall take a handful of it as a memorial portion and burn it on the altar on top of the food offerings presented to the Lord. It is a sin offering. In this way the priest will make atonement for them for any of these sins they have committed, and they will be forgiven. The rest of the offering will belong to the priest, as in the case of the grain offering." (Leviticus 5)

Based on the passage, Fulton determined that God told him to bake or rather burn bread as a sacrifice—a sin offering. After all, we didn't have any small lambs or doves lying around. Being obedient, he marched into the kitchen and launched into a process that resulted in a stinky burning flour mixture billowing out into the dining room. Archie was playing outside and came in the back door, stopped, and announced, "That smells delicious!"

Out of the mouths of babes.

I knew in that moment my son was indeed a prophet. After that experience, Fulton launched into yet another career perfecting bread baking using mash from a local whiskey distillery to create the best sourdough I've ever tasted. Word of this special bread spread like wildfire and sales through the distillery led to an opportunity to become the bread chef at the Franklin Bakehouse, a new restaurant in our small town. He has become an icon in our town for his efforts. He is now working and teaching young people to make artisan bread. He is able to turn everything he's ever done into a ministry, and it is true even at the bakehouse. He regularly cooks for these young folks who don't have local family. It is another opportunity to share his skills and faith with the next generation.

The lesson learned is that being obedient, even if it doesn't make sense or feel comfortable in the moment, is a critical part of living a godly, happy life. Obedience generates blessings.

I'm still a work in progress, but we both have most certainly been blessed by the goodness of God.

> "Anyone who listens to my teaching and follows it is wise, like a person who builds a house on solid rock." (Matthew 7:24 NLT)

Miracle 11

Women of the Bible

In March of 2019, after years of discussion and planning, we were finally making a pilgrimage to Israel. For ten years, I wanted to make this journey but the timing, the investment, and one hundred other factors just had not lined up. Fulton was so excited. We were committed to the same church and really wanted to go with our pastor and his wife to experience Israel with people we love. The tour was led by Amir Tsfarti, a messianic Jew, historian, author, and major in the Israeli Defense Force. Amir is also an amazing storyteller. We were set for the trip of a lifetime, the opportunity literally to walk where Jesus walked, and see what Jesus saw narrated by two men we both deeply respect.

For years, we heard stories about Israel, but being there live and in person was a dream come true. After a flight through London and on to Tel Aviv, we were both tired but thrilled to begin our exploration of this amazing country. Israel is the size of New Jersey, and yet, topographically, it is like combining Colorado, Hawaii, Arizona, and New York into a single long thin nation brimming with God's people and prosperity. My impression was that it was all desert, mountainous and rugged. I'd been to Saudi Arabia five years prior, so no doubt that was coloring my preconceived notion of the Jewish state. However, that impression could not have been further from the truth. Israel is lush, green, gorgeous, and bountiful. It wasn't always this way, prior to the British once again returning the Jewish homeland to the people. After the brutality of the Holocaust, God's people returned to their home, determined to build a successful nation that was self-reliant and independent. More importantly, they made a commitment to protect themselves, forever pouring their collective lives into bringing a barren landscape back to life. With God's help, it was accomplished, beyond their wildest dreams. Fruit and food grow everywhere, rivers and oceans are clean and filled with fish and marine life and natural resources. A promise fulfilled.

> They began to return to Judah from the places
> to which they had fled. They stopped at Mizpah
> to meet with Gedaliah and then went into the
> Judean countryside to gather a great harvest of
> grapes and other crops. (Jeremiah 40:12 NLT)

For the first time in a decade, I was willing to turn my phone off, leave work behind, and totally focus on being present. I didn't want to miss one thing or one word from our awesome hosts. We began our tour in Tel Aviv, staying in an amazing hotel overlooking the ocean. From there, we traveled to Joppa and the Caesarea to literally hear our pastor preach in the same amphitheater where Paul defended himself as a citizen of Rome in front of Governor Felix. It was thrilling. From there, we headed north to the Sea of Galilea, a large lake where the apostles made their living as fishermen. We visited a museum where we saw a fishing boat dating back to the time of Christ that had been found in the mud, fully intact. Everywhere we turned, Bible stories were given flesh and substance. After waking up at sunrise to see light spread over this gorgeous lake, we headed to a tour of the headwaters of the Jordan and then on to the Golan Heights. I was enthralled with the history, both ancient and modern. I love to see, touch, and hear about historic events, especially when shared by great theologians and historians. There was a new sign on the Golan Heights, where you can still see bunkers that said "Trump Heights," recognizing the president's support for the nation of Israel.

From there, we headed to the end of the lake to the town of Magdala, as in Mary Magdalene. This was a port town, where fishermen brought their catch to sell. At the time of Jesus, it was bustling and included a large synagogue. The Catholic church was intent on building a visitors' center and hotel at the edge of the lake and began construction in 2009. At that time, no one could have imagined what would be unearthed just beneath the surface. As workers began to dig the foundation for the guesthouse, they discovered a first-century synagogue where Jesus taught. Inside the synagogue, they also found the Magdala Stone, a discovery many archaeologists call the most significant archaeological find in the past fifty years. It is a stone box that once held the Torah and has the oldest carving of a menorah ever found.

As archaeologists continued to dig, they discovered an entire first-century Jewish town lying just below the surface. With only 10 percent of it uncovered, the hometown of Mary Magdalene offers pilgrims the experience to literally walk where Jesus taught and to connect with the first-century life of Jesus's earliest followers.

For me, the most interesting thing about Magdala was meeting Father Eamon Kelly, an Irish priest with an amazing brogue who has become a close friend of our pastor. Father Kelly oversees what has become an interesting and important Holy Land site including a gorgeous church dedicated to women of the Bible. As a recovering Catholic, I found Father Kelly's passion for Jesus and history were warm and comforting. His authenticity and intensity were moving as he shared everything behind this lovely chapel and the artisans who donated their talent to create gorgeous mosaics in the small side chapels on the main floor. The large chapel looks out over the Sea of Galilee and includes an altar shaped like a fishing boat from the time of Christ. It is lovely, appropriate, and filled with the spirit. Before we left, Father Kelly asked us to follow him down to the lower level because there was a crowd in the main sanctuary. We obediently trailed behind him, down stone steps to a room with an ancient stone floor and curved wall with a fresco covering every inch that is both striking and beautiful. It is the feet of Jesus and the apostles with a women's hand reaching out to the hem of His garment. It honors the woman with the bleeding issue whose faith healed her.

Father Kelly asked if there was anyone in the room who needed to pray for their daughters. I nearly fell off the stone I was sitting on. I quickly raised my hand, and the good father asked me to stand up, give him my phone, and reach out toward the fresco. He asked me to move into place and then took pictures while he spoke about miracles. I began to cry and feel the Spirt of God fall on all of us. I was a mess, totally and completely wrecked. I know God heard my pleading, the cry of my heart. I felt like I was heard and understood. It was a very special moment.

As we moved on, we were also able to visit the Wailing Wall in Jerusalem. I didn't understand the significance of this sacred place. After the destruction of the temple at the hands of the Romans in March of AD 70, the Jews were banned from their holiest of holy temples. To this day, the only access they have is the exterior of the Western Wall. Daily, people come from all over the world, adding their prayers to small pieces of paper then inserting them into the cracks between the giant stones. Two prayers were added by my hand, one for my daughters and one for friends who had been trying to have a baby for more than a decade.

One prayer has already been answered: Rivers, the miracle baby was born sixteen months ago and is doing very well. We are still waiting for a cure for my daughters, but I believe that those prayers will also be answered.

> Jesus turned around, and when he saw her he said, "Daughter, be encouraged! Your faith has made you well." And the woman was healed at that moment. (Matthew 9: 22 NLT)

Miracle 12

The Clinical Trial Sign

June 2020 was the height of the COVID-19 pandemic. Despite that, my middle child Lauren, just twenty-four, was determined to complete a clinical trial for the first ever biologic treatment for Fredrich's Ataxia. The conditions were brutal: ten days trapped in a small space on the third floor of an office building in a small town in New Jersey. I will admit that the thought made me claustrophobic but, if she was willing, then who was I to say no. The process included pre-trial testing and my first COVID test, which was less than comfortable (there were no spit options at that time). We were able to fly on a private jet, covered by the biotech sponsor—the one good thing about the COVID restrictions. At the private airport outside of Nashville, we were joined by two sisters who had grown up within miles of my girls. That alone was surprising. The girls were in their early to mid-thirties and both were married with two sons each. Their voices were affected as was their ability to walk, but with walkers and amazing attitudes, they quickly calmed any concerns Lauren had about living a big, full life, even with FA. This was an adventure, and they were looking forward to it, their excitement refreshing.

As we raced across the sky toward New Jersey, the sisters and Lauren quickly became friends. They had wonderful attitudes, and I said a quick prayer, thankful Lauren now had mentors who were living their lives, happily married, and raising children. That did my mother's heart so much good.

Previously, I had been with my older child to a few visits for another clinical trial at Emory in Atlanta. Matilda's clinical trial was medication based and done remotely for the most part, with a check-in required every few months. Each visit, after a day of testing, she was free to enjoy a nice dinner and relax at a local hotel. These visits had become a "get away" for her and her husband.

COVID changed everything. For Lauren, participants and their support people were required to remain together, locked away from other people during the entire process. The group was made up of twelve participants ranging in age from eighteen to seventy. We all had private rooms connected to our loved ones through a shared bathroom. Other than the internet being weak, and the food leaving much to be desired, we were comfortable. Lauren and I brought seven games and became the leaders of an evening game table that broke down barriers and kept everyone in good spirits.

This trial was phase one, meaning it was the first time that the medication would be injected into humans. It was also double blind, so not everyone would get the actual medication. Although the risks were real, moving the process forward was critical to getting to real treatment. The medication was frataxin, the protein my daughters could no longer make due to the genetic defect both their father and I carry. If the frataxin could be tolerated, the hope would be that a shot every few days would increase their levels to something closer to normal. This would then reduce or slow the decline of this condition and maybe even repair some of the damage. Just a single shot, however, was not going to radically change anything. However, it was a step toward a real biologic solution. The hope is that this would work like insulin for a diabetic. The scientific challenge is that the protein had to penetrate the cellular membrane in order to boost the energy of the cell—not a simple process. The mRNA technology made popular by the COVID vaccine is the same technology deployed to achieve success in the trial in which we were about to participate.

I wasn't sure I'd be able to tell if Lauren received the medicine or if we'd have any idea if the medicine crossed the cell membrane. I started to pray for a sign, some indication that the results were positive. This trial, if successful, would be followed by a multi-dose test. If both were successful, then we'd be very close to an open label trial. That meant Lauren would get access to this miracle drug for two years for free. Longer term, we are hoping for a genetic therapy (meaning one shot and the software update would repair the broken gene) allowing her to have nearly normal frataxin production. This was the next best thing: a medication that gave us time for the more impactful "one and done" treatment.

It's a lot to mull over, ponder, and consider. Alone in a room that appeared more insane asylum than hotel, I had much to reflect on since the diagnosis nearly six years ago. We were also close to Lauren's twenty-fifth birthday and I asked the clinical trial team to help me celebrate her day. Unorthodox as it was, birthdays still matter.

The night before "dosing day," I decided to initiate some "collective bargaining." The food was not great and, given our predicament, I suggested we be able to select what we wanted from a new menu and demanded Chick-fil-A (or as we call it, Jesus Chicken) be added to the mix. They asked us all to fill out our choice on paper with some pens. Writing is a challenge for those living with Friederichs's Ataxia. However, each participant was able to make his or her choice known and the excitement over better food was palpable.

Lauren was buoyant and moved through the pre-dosing activities with ease. A few members had received a pre-pre-dosing a two days prior to ensure that the remaining cohort would be safe. One of the men became ill, which made me and everyone else nervous, but we were all committed to seeing the process through. After the dosing, which they would not allow me to attend, Lauren rested comfortably and was just a bit nauseous. I knew she had received the actual dose—a prayer answered. Fortunately, by dinner she was feeling well enough to eat something. We again filled out our choices by hand. I heard her call for me from her room, "Mom, get in here and look at this!" She showed me her handwriting and I could immediately see that it was markedly different from the day before. "Mom, it looks like it did in high school!" We both just stared at the words she'd written on the piece of paper. Such a small thing, but not small at all.

We immediately searched for the lead physician, a kind, older Jewish man who had shared some of his story with us about adopting children and wanting to make the world a better place. I said, "Hey, check this out!" and the good doctor came over to Lauren's bed and reviewed the before and after handwriting sample. He looked at us, and with tears in his eyes, said, "I never get to see impact like this." I knew in that moment we got our "God nod;" it had worked and, from that moment, I didn't worry about the results of this clinical trial or the next. The hope that this small miracle gave both of us and her sister was invaluable. We ended the trial with cake and flowers provided by the care team to usher in her 25th year on the planet. We were so happy to return home, but it was well worth every minute of suffering. I even called ahead and ordered pizza and wine to be delivered to the private airport hangar so the group could have one more celebration before we all flew back to our lives.

The sisters had done something else for Lauren. They told her to get a walker, the kind they both used, and not to give up too soon on walking. They also let her know that being married and having children was not impossible, despite the diagnosis. This was tremendous insight from an unexpected source (anyone other than me).

We flew home filled with hope. The next clinical trial cohort involved multiple doses (shots) of the frataxin every few days over a twenty-day period, requiring participants to stay in lock-down for nearly a month. After speaking to the trial coordinator, we were told that because Lauren had participated in the very first human trial, she was eligible for the open label study. Open label is the part of the clinical trial process when dosing has been tested and a protocol created. It can last two years, and the participants receive access to the medication for free. We heard from some of the other participants that they were going to participate in the second dosing trial. No one can share information about the trial process or results (if they are even witness to them). It took several months, but the biotech creators of the frataxin and proprietary delivery strategy necessary to get the protein into the cellular level launched a press release. It detailed the positive impact of both trials and the intent to move forward with the open label phase.

We were ecstatic, as you might imagine! I knew that the phase two trial was going to work based on what we had personally experienced. That was not stressful for me, but waiting to hear about the open label phase has been extremely stressful. Almost a year after we returned from New Jersey, we received bad news. The FDA stopped the forward motion because a monkey died. Being a data-centric person, I had to look up the weight of the animal and how much of the frataxin they'd given him. After some research, I determined that a seven-pound monkey who received forty times the dose that Lauren had received over an extended period of time had died. My kid weighs 125 pounds, so that translates to nearly 700 times the dose if we're talking apples to apples.

As a parent with two children who have a life-threatening disease, you can imagine my angst. During the COVID pandemic, a clinical trial that had been successful in humans was put on hold over the demise of a very small anthropoid. It all seemed so unfair! My prayers were no longer gratitude but anger. I was concerned about how long this small biotech company could survive if the open label didn't commence soon. I had friends in the industry investigate the FDA feedback. I did what I do: I tried to control a completely uncontrollable situation.

Patience is a virtue, one that I have very little of unfortunately. In the interim, Lauren continued to work hard at a new job, expanding her graphic design and social media skill set. We tried not to talk about it constantly but continued to interact with the trial participants through email and social media. We also reached out to FARA (Friedreich's Ataxia Research Alliance) to stay on top of our trial and any others. A month became a year and then nearly a year and a half. The new date for the open label was moved from fall of 2021 to 2022. We waited and went back to our lives.

In October of 2021, while I was talking to Lauren about a project her team was working on for my company, she started to cry. When my daughters call me crying, I rarely think that there is good news attached to the tears. In this case, they were tears of joy. She had received an email letting her know she was in the open label trial, and it was going forward.

We don't know, at this point, if it will slow her decline or if there is a real possibility of gaining back function that has been lost. However, this was much more than a drop of hope, I know in my heart that it will buy us time for something genetic that will really address the underlying issue. Once again, the God of the universe let me know He sees me, my husband, and our children. We are not alone in our suffering. Her sister Matilda had recently suggested that they both pray every day. The Bible says that we must ask for what we want and need. Knowing that my children are asking in unison provides me with tremendous hope.

Literally a few weeks before the end of 2021, Lauren was communicating with a man who had been in her cohort as well the second cohort. He had been a chiropractor, but the disease has ravaged him, affecting his speech considerably and his ability to move. He had a small scooter type contraption he sat on and pushed with his feet, providing some exercise and the ability to freely move around. The window into my daughter's future was frightening, but he was such a kind spirit and was always in motion to the point that his disabilities were not the focus. When you participate in a clinical trial, you agree not to share anything before, during, or after to avoid impacting results. However, nearly six months had passed from the conclusion of the second cohort, which involved twenty days of shots. There had been a press release suggesting that things had gone well but offered no details. Once again, Lauren called me, her voice shaky with emotion. She shared that this man had messaged her and said that he once again got the medicine and that his voice was fully restored. He was also able to walk a bit for the first time in a decade. Even more incredible, his voice was still perfect even though some time had passed. This news was miraculous, amazing, and thoroughly wonderful!

Hope is such a precious commodity. I believe God gives us peeks into heavenly truth and possibility to remind us He is in charge, and He cares. Ultimately, my children will run and do cartwheels in heaven if they are not cured here on earth. One day, they will be fully restored.

The incredible gift of hope can benefit us no matter what we are facing. I know this to be true from real lived experience.

May the God of the Universe send you miracles, messages, and moments designed just for you. May you see them with the wonder and majesty in which they were intended—the precious faith of a child.

Never give up. God is real and present, and you are not alone. He sees you and is cheering you on through whatever you are facing. Call His name, share your pain and suffering, and ask for guidance.

Persevere. Let your faith be made pure by His eternal promises.

Never lose heart.

> In his kindness God called you to share in his eternal glory by means of Christ Jesus. So after you have suffered a little while, he will restore, support, and strengthen you, and he will place you on a firm foundation. (1 Peter 5:10 NLT)

Epilogue

I began writing this book three years ago. It was a promise I made to myself, and the author and finisher of our faith. As 2023 began, I vowed that this was the year I would publish my story. I love to read. When I become familiar with characters, it creates real relationship and begs the question, "Well, what happened?" For those who share that same thirst for transparency, I thought I'd add an epilogue to provide an update on all things Franco.

Archie will graduate from college in just a few short months. The end of an era has arrived and, if I'm being honest, I'm not ready to be an empty nester. Nevertheless, time marches on no matter how much I would like to freeze it. That chubby baby is now my "man baby." He remains a good boy, caring, thoughtful, and deeply empathetic. He writes beautiful songs and is ready to release his first album. The years worrying about his sisters have been hard on him, but I know he is grateful that he can now be a help to them and a friend. The Christian high school I fought to send him to was most certainly the right decision. He is on his own journey, but I know that he knows who he is and whose he is.

Lauren is now twenty-six and has launched a successful new side hustle as a stand-up comedian. She calls it "sit-down comedy" and I'm amazed at how quickly things have taken off for her. She has been invited to several comedy festivals, including Ashville and Atlanta, and is a regular at the big comedy club in Nashville. She heads to Los Angeles in May for several shows and has been asked to be a delegate to the 2023 Annual Ataxia Conference in Las Vegas. Her comedy has become a platform to inspire others who struggle with neurologic conditions. She does not let her disability define her. She owns her own home, runs a graphic design business she started on her own, and she truly is very, very funny. She takes a few shots at her mother, but I can't blame her. I suppose that is just part of the amends process. Given that the humor gene comes from the Franco side, I'm just fine with that.

Matilda is now thirty and is working on a PhD in organizational behavior. She has exceeded all academic expectations and often calls to ask me (or rather challenge me) on the fine points of running a company. Her clinical trial, begun at Emory five years ago, concluded on Rare Disease Day, February 28, 2023, when the first medication for any form of muscular dystrophy was passed by the FDA. We both cried as the press release validated what I knew in my heart. The medication has slowed the progression by about 50 percent. Although she is four years older than her sister, she is doing very well, and her voice remains strong. Her focus for her dissertation is integrating those with physical disabilities into the workforce. She also helps others with her condition to develop resumes and find meaningful work. She is a champion for those with no voice in both recovery and disability circles. True to that prophetess in Nicaragua, her life is impacting many and there is a long road ahead.

Fulton is once again a pastor after a few years baking bread during COVID. There were many days when I headed out to jog to find someone at the end of our walkway asking me, "Is this where the breadman lives?" He loved baking and working with young people, teaching them how to make sourdough and even focaccia (he strives to be an Italian as part of the Franco tribe). However, the Lord has called him back to duty and at sixty-seven years old, he is the senior statesman at our church. As the Connections Pastor, he is in his element, supporting those who have need in our local community and building and expanding small groups, creating greater connection within our church. He was even able to create a video at the church on a series about miracles detailing the healing he experienced for his lung condition. We continue to receive wonderful feedback about the lives his story has impacted.

It seems we have come full circle in a journey that nearly spans the amount of time invested in my first marriage. Our fifteenth-year anniversary arrives this July. That too is very hard to believe. Through the difficulty and the tears, we have walked forward together and are committed to the long haul. God knew best and I am grateful every morning that I was obedient to his sage advice.

I still run, perhaps a bit slower but just as consistently. As I head out of my house, I thank the God of the universe for every breath and every step. I will run until my daughters run or I leave this world for the next. I made that commitment to my children, and I intend, God willing, to keep it.

Bibliography

Metaxas, Eric. *Miracles: What They Are, Why They Happen, and How They Can Change Your Life*. New York: Penguin, 2014.

Printed in the United States
by Baker & Taylor Publisher Services